SUPPOSING
Bleak House

VICTORIAN LITERATURE AND CULTURE SERIES
Jerome J. McGann and Herbert F. Tucker, Editors

SUPPOSING
Bleak House

JOHN O. JORDAN

UNIVERSITY OF VIRGINIA PRESS
CHARLOTTESVILLE AND LONDON

University of Virginia Press
© 2011 by the Rector and Visitors of the University of Virginia
All rights reserved
Printed in the United States of America on acid-free paper

First published 2011
First paperback edition published 2013
ISBN 978-0-8139-3444-0 (paper)

1 3 5 7 9 8 6 4 2

The Library of Congress has cataloged the hardcover edition as follows:
LIBRARY OF CONGRESS CATALOGING-IN-PUBLICATION DATA
Jordan, John O.
  Supposing Bleak House / John O. Jordan.
    p.   cm.—(Victorian literature and culture series)
  Includes bibliographical references and index.
  ISBN 978-0-8139-3074-9 (acid-free paper)—ISBN 978-0-8139-3092-3 (e-book)
  1. Dickens, Charles, 1812–1870. Bleak House. I. Title.
  PR4556.J67 2010
  823'.8—dc22

2010020833

Unless otherwise noted, all illustrations are by Hablot K. Browne, etchings from original serial parts of *Bleak House*, 1852–53. (Courtesy of the Department of Special Collections, Stanford University Libraries)

For Jane

CONTENTS

	List of Illustrations	viii
	Acknowledgments	ix
1	Voice	1
2	Illustration	26
3	Psychoanalysis	44
4	Endings	67
5	Dickens	87
6	Specters	113
	Epilogue: Christmas	141
	Appendix: The Ghost in *Bleak House*	147
	Notes	161
	Bibliography	171
	Index	179

ILLUSTRATIONS

1. "The appointed time" — 29
2. "Mr. Guppy's Desolation" — 30
3. "The little church in the park" — 32
4. "Consecrated ground" — 34
5. "The Little old Lady" — 36
6. "The Ghost's Walk" — 37
7. "Lady Dedlock in the Wood" — 39
8. "The Young Man of the name of Guppy" — 51
9. "The Mausoleum at Chesney Wold" — 81
10. "Sunset in the long Drawing-room at Chesney Wold" — 116
11. "Becky's second appearance in the character of Clytemnestra" — 151
12. "The Mausoleum at Chesney Wold," working drawing — 153
13. "The Mausoleum at Chesney Wold," drawing, 1853? — 155
14. "The Mausoleum at Chesney Wold," lithographic transfer?, first bound edition — 157
15. "The Mausoleum at Chesney Wold," etching from 1938 edition (reprinted 2005, Nonesuch edition) — 158
16. "Rose Maylie and Oliver" — 159

ACKNOWLEDGMENTS

LONG CONTEMPLATED, THIS BOOK WOULD NOT ALLOW ITSELF to be written until it was ready. When the time came, it offered itself with unstinting generosity. Lengthy incubation in this case entails great indebtedness. I owe thanks in the first instance to Murray Baumgarten and Ed Eigner, who brought me along when they had the idea of starting a Dickens research group at the University of California. To Murray in particular, the Dickens Project's founding director and my longtime co-conspirator in all things Dickensian, I owe a debt of gratitude for colleagueship that extends over four decades and that includes many conversations about *Bleak House*.

An early version of chapter 1 was presented at the 2001 Dickens Universe gathering in Santa Cruz. I am grateful to friends, students, and colleagues for their positive response on that occasion and to delegates at the 2009 "Uneasy Pleasures" conference in Jerusalem, where I presented a later version of this chapter. The book's appendix appeared in the March 2010 issue of *Dickens Quarterly* and is reprinted here with the kind permission of the journal's editor, David Paroissien.

To Bob Newsom and Hilary Schor, two passionate, expert readers of *Bleak House*, I owe special thanks for their long friendship and for innumerable exchanges about Esther and about Dickens. So many of the ideas that appear in these pages first took shape in conversations between the three of us that it is sometimes difficult for me to know to whom they properly belong, though of course I bear ultimate responsibility for the words on the page. Bob read the entire manuscript, offered many useful suggestions, and was especially helpful in sharpening my understanding of the novel's illustrations.

Others who read the manuscript and provided useful advice include Bob Patten, who took valuable time away from his own research to check first editions of the novel at the Rice University library; Dick Stein, whose encouragement came at a crucial moment; Lou Breger and Jon Varese, each of whom saved me from embarrassing mistakes; and Tim Peltason, whose detailed comments helped improve my argument at several points. Helen Hauser provided important research assistance in London. Lunch conversations with Michael Warren, Gary Miles, and Galia Benziman advanced my work in ways of which they may not be fully aware.

A series of informal study sessions with JoAnn and Greg Bellow proved valuable in developing my ideas about psychoanalysis. Even when Greg and I disagreed—especially when we disagreed—our exchanges forced me to clarify my thinking and look for further evidence to explain what I was trying to say. The book is better as a result of our dialogue. At a later stage, Estelle Shane gave me incisive comments on some of the psychoanalytic ideas I was trying to work out.

Without the assistance of libraries and librarians, this project would have been impossible to complete. I am grateful to the staff of McHenry Library at the University of California, Santa Cruz, for timely help in processing interlibrary loan requests. For assistance in locating illustrations and for granting permission to reproduce them, I thank John Mustain and Mattie Taormina at the Stanford University Libraries, Katharine Chandler and Joseph Shemtov at the Free Library of Philadelphia, Moira Fitzgerald at the Beinecke Rare Book and Manuscript Library, Yale University, and David Marshall of Duckworth Publishers. At several points my research has been supported by grants from the Academic Senate Committee on Research at the University of California, Santa Cruz. I appreciate the committee's confidence in my work.

The memory of two people who will never know how much I owe to them looms large in the background of this book. One is my mother,

ACKNOWLEDGMENTS

Mary Hamilton Thompson Orr Jordan, whose presence can be felt on almost every page. The other is Sally Ledger, whose untimely death in early 2009, just as a draft of this book was nearing completion, left a large hole in the community of nineteenth-century scholars of which I am a part. The importance for me of Sally's work on Dickens is especially evident in chapter 6.

To JoAnna Rottke, the Dickens Project's incomparable coordinator, and to Jay Olson, computing assistant at UC Santa Cruz, I am grateful for help in preparing the manuscript for publication. To Cathie Brettschneider at the University of Virginia Press, I am thankful for many courtesies, for her patience in answering questions, and for her faith in this project. Thanks go as well to Colleen Romick Clark, herself a Victorianist, for her supportive and sharp-eyed copyediting.

My greatest debt is to my wife, Jane, who shares her life with me and from whom I have absorbed much that is in this book. Her love and confidence in me made it possible for *Supposing "Bleak House"* to be written.

SUPPOSING
Bleak House

1
VOICE

I TOO HAVE A GREAT DEAL OF DIFFICULTY IN BEGINNING TO write my portion of these pages. I know that I find *Bleak House* to be the most powerful of all of Dickens's novels, and yet I fear that I will never be able to explain adequately to anyone else or to myself why it exerts such a strong hold over me. I know that I have been reading *Bleak House* for nearly forty years and that each time I reach the point where Esther discovers what she has not quite yet allowed herself to realize is her mother's body lying outside the miserable graveyard, each time she lifts the heavy head, puts the long dank hair aside, turns the face, and recognizes that "it was my mother, cold and dead," I weep. I weep in part because this scene vividly evokes the memory of my own mother's death. I weep also because the words of disavowal that Esther uses to fend off the terrible knowledge—calling the female figure before her "the mother of the dead child," words at once mistaken and yet truer than she knows—these words resonate closely with certain crucial facts of my mother's life (and hence of my own), the loss of her first-born child (my older brother) at the age of two and a half, and her death thirty-six years later only one day before the anniversary of that great sadness.

I weep in addition, of course, because the simple and yet chilling words with which chapter 59 comes to a close are so magnificently orchestrated, the narrative voice so powerful and pure. Dickens, or rather Esther—for it is to her that I wish to credit the writing in this and the other chapters that she narrates—slows down the action of discovery into its component parts, each within a separate clause, forcing the reader to experience syntactically the recognition that she at once resists and, unconsciously and in retrospect, knows to be inevitable. After so many chapters, and so many words, the stark monosyllables—"long dank hair," "turned the face," "cold and dead"—strike with unusual force. One of the finest things in all of Dickens, this chapter ending (which also ends the penultimate monthly number) is the thematic and emotional climax of the novel. It not only brings to an end the hallucinatory chase sequence involving Esther and Detective Bucket that occupies most of monthly numbers 17 and 18; it also provides closure of a sort to three important and related strands in Esther's inner journey: her quest for a stable, coherent self, for reunion with her mother, and for understanding of the mystery of her origins. What it does for her as narrator, what it omits and leaves unresolved, I shall have more to say about later in this essay.

The difficulty I experience in writing about *Bleak House* derives not only from my personal associations to the novel or from the worry that I will be unable to convey the special feelings that reading it awakens in me. The difficulty derives equally from my awareness of the novel's critical history and my concern, after so many other critics have written so well about it, that I have little new to add. The novel's critical history weighs all the more heavily upon me when I recall the leading role that friends and colleagues in the University of California Dickens Project have played in contributing to it, from Robert Newsom's pathbreaking 1977 monograph to the excellent subsequent discussions by Lawrence Frank, Albert D. Hutter, Fred Kaplan, Helena Michie, Hilary Schor, Audrey Jaffe, Barbara Gottfried, Marcia Goodman, John Glavin, Garrett Stewart, Gordon Bigelow, James Buzard, Richard L. Stein, Robert Patten, Robert Tracy, Sally Ledger, and many others.[1]

The reading of *Bleak House* that most closely parallels my own and that I currently hold in highest esteem is the chapter that another friend, Carolyn Dever, devotes to the novel in her excellent study *Death and the Mother from Dickens to Freud*. Like Dever, my interest in the novel focuses chiefly on the Esther narrative and on the melancholy fascination with the mother that lies at the heart of Esther's autobiographical account. Like Dever, I find that in many ways the novel anticipates psychoanalytic explanations of the formation of subjectivity and that it is usefully read alongside and through the lens of psychoanalytic theory.[2] Dever writes eloquently of the ways in which Esther's ambivalent search for the mother structures her autobiography and produces uncanny displacements and repetitions in her narrative. She tracks with exceptional acuteness the recurring fantasies of dead mother and dead child that haunt Esther's imagination and that establish her as "a *ghostly* presence, a living absence, within her own autobiography."[3] She gives particularly fine readings of Esther's relationship with her doll and of the painful reunion scene between Esther and Lady Dedlock in chapter 36, showing how Esther in this scene is forced to acquiesce in her own abandonment by a mother who no sooner reveals herself as living than she commands her daughter to "evermore consider her as dead."[4] Although "not technically rejected here," Dever writes, "[Esther] has had rejection dictated to her."[5] In effect, the scene of reunion reenacts the original trauma of birth and maternal abandonment, once again leaving mother and daughter symbolically dead to each other and yet condemned to remain alive, only this time with more certain evidence of the mother's now conscious and deliberate betrayal.

My reading of the novel differs from that of Dever not so much in the way we view Esther's character and psychology as in the greater emphasis I give to questions of voice and temporality in her narrative. My focus is on Esther as narrator and what it means for her to tell the story of her life, looking back on it as a married woman from the perspective of seven years. At the risk of oversimplifying, I might say that I am more interested in Esther Woodcourt than in Esther Summerson, although this distinction overlooks the confusion of subject positions that results from her use of the first-person pronoun together with past-tense verbs that lack temporal specificity. The pronoun "I" and even the proper name "Esther" are ambiguous. They can refer either to Esther the character at different points in her life or to the Esther who writes her "portion of these pages"—or sometimes to all of these. The signifiers slide; utterance and enunciation blur, merging past and present selves in ways that often render the distinction impossible.[6]

Esther's account in chapter 18 of seeing Lady Dedlock in the church is a good example of how this blurring occurs. It is an uncanny moment—not the first that Esther records, but one of the most important. After describing the unsettling effect that the sight of Lady Dedlock's face had upon her, she writes, "*I*—*I*, little Esther Summerson, the child who lived a life apart, and on whose birthday there was no rejoicing—seemed to arise before my own eyes, evoked out of the past by some power in this fashionable lady" (292). What bears emphasizing here is the way in which three distinct times and three separate selves converge in the space of only a few words: the Esther who saw Lady Dedlock in the church, the memory of a younger self that emerged spontaneously at that time, but also the Esther who, in writing about this moment, reexperiences it in the present. The double (and italicized) pronouns, together with the proper name, delineate, at the same time that they conflate, these three identities, anticipating Jo's astonished question in chapter 31 (in a very different context): "Is there *three* of 'em then?" (493).

The structure of repetition that characterizes Esther's narrative and that produces so many uncanny moments in her text derives from two main sources. In its simplest form it is a result of the fact that she writes in the past tense. "Narrative," writes Peter Brooks, "always makes the implicit claim to be in a state of repetition, as a going over again of a ground already covered: a *sjužet* repeating the *fabula*, as the detective retraces the tracks of the criminal."[7] Retrospective narration necessarily involves discursive repetition, but retrospection also has other potentially interesting consequences. Most notably, for my purposes, it entails foreknowledge on the part of the retrospective narrator of as yet unnarrated events. In *Bleak House,* this means that Esther Woodcourt knows from the beginning everything that will happen to Esther Summerson. It means that she knows and remembers the reunion scene narrated in chapter 36, even as she begins to write, and it means that she always sees the corpse of the dead mother waiting for her at the end of her journey through the stormy night. The foreknowledge that results from narrative hindsight at times disrupts Esther's linear presentation of her story, producing detemporalized, associative connections in which the memory of events that remain to be told impinges on the present moment of her narrating. The result is a complex layering of temporalities that adds to the uncanny effect of the narrative as a whole.[8]

To say that Esther already knows the story of her past and repeats it discursively in her narrative, while accurate, does not give a complete picture of her role as narrator. There are things about her past that Esther knows but does not understand; there are things she is unaware that she knows and that she is therefore incapable of telling; and there are things that she knows but does not *want* to know. In a sense, then, we can say that her story is still to a great extent unknown to her. In retelling it, she is in effect re-experiencing it as she writes, and this re-experience has the potential to shed new light, for her as well as for the reader, on events that have already happened. Part of Esther's goal in writing is thus to understand not the facts of her life but their meaning. To adopt Brooks's metaphor, we might say that Esther here is the detective of her own life, sifting and interpreting her past for clues that will help her better to understand and come to terms with it in the present. At the same time, some of the knowledge that she acquires by writing about herself and some of the memories that she reawakens in going back over the past are painful to her, and she often tries to avoid thinking about them, shaking her mental keys and taking herself dutifully to task with the familiar refrain "Esther, Esther, Esther."[9] If Esther is a detective, she is often a reluctant one.

Esther's efforts to resist painful knowledge about herself do not always succeed, however, and it is the return of these thoughts, often against her will, that is the second main source of repetition in her narrative. Many of the uncanny repetitions in Esther's narrative arise out of her unconscious mind and derive from the pressure of forgotten or half-remembered events on her present awareness. As both character and narrator, she is haunted by an upsurge of strange, unbidden memories that take her back again and again to the earliest moments of her life. Associated with her doll, her godmother, and especially her mother's face (all versions perhaps of the same lost original), these memory fragments cluster around an experience that she can never consciously recall but about which she has many fears, doubts, and fantasies: the moment of her birth. Esther reports that she first began to wonder about the circumstances of her birth when, as a young girl, she realized that there was no rejoicing at home and no holiday at school on her birthday. She writes that on one particularly melancholy recurrence of that day she broke down in tears and asked her godmother, "Did mama die on my birthday?" (30). Thus, from early on, Esther imagines her birthday as a deathday. She fears that the mother whom she never knew as a child died in giving birth to her and that she may therefore somehow be responsible for the mother's death. Much later, in chapter 36, she reports having learned from Lady Dedlock's letter the "true" story of her birth: that she had "not been abandoned by my mother," that the godmother of her childhood, "discovering signs of life in me when I had been laid aside as dead," had reared her in rigid secrecy and concealed her existence from the baby's mother, who began to suspect that her daughter was still alive only after their unexpected encounter in the church (583).

The story is plausible enough. Moreover, it finds corroboration (in chapters told by the other narrator) in the evidence that Mrs. Chadband, the former "Mrs. Rachael" of the godmother's household, gives to Inspector Bucket in chapter 54, as well as in Lady Dedlock's melodramatic soliloquy at the end of chapter 29: "O my child, my child! Not dead in the first hours of her life, as my cruel sister told me; but sternly nurtured by her, after she had renounced me and my name! O my child, O my child!" (469). Alongside and in competition with this account, however, Esther retains the fantasy not only that her mother died in giving birth to her but also that she herself died and, more horribly yet, that her mother wished her dead, deliberately abandoned her, may even have buried her body within hours after she was born. Although contradicted by the evidence of her senses (since both she and her mother are manifestly alive), this phantasmatic, nightmarish counternarrative nevertheless persists in Esther's unconscious, rising sometimes almost to the level of conscious memory and producing strange narrative effects, including the impression that she and her mother are ghosts haunting each other, both of them alive and at the same time dead.

Horrifying as well as fascinating, these thoughts alternately repel and attract her. She is drawn irresistibly toward them, but also does her best to avoid them. The alternation between these contradictory feeling states, what Dickens elsewhere famously called "the attraction of repulsion,"[10] results in a curious syncopation in Esther's narrative, a zigzag rhythm in her prose that she repeats literally on the occasion of her reunion with Ada after recovering from the illness that scars her face. Just as, on that occasion, she first runs eagerly down the road to greet her friend and then retreats shyly to the safety of her room, so in her narrative she vacillates awkwardly between passages of direct, sometimes powerful openness and moments of coy reticence and evasion.

At times, Esther seems to be a much more knowing and self-aware narrator than critics generally give her credit for being, although one must read carefully in order to pick up the subtle, often oblique signs of this awareness. Consider, for example, her report in chapter 36 of reading the letter from Lady Dedlock that purports to tell the truth about Esther's origins. Dever correctly emphasizes the devastating implications that these revelations have for Esther at the time, but she does not point out some of the small lexical and rhetorical cues that indicate Esther's subsequent and, I think, more critical response. "Safe in my own room," Esther writes, "I read the letter. I clearly derived from it— and that was much then—that I had not been abandoned by my mother" (583). Whenever Esther interrupts herself, as she does here with the clause set off by dashes, we need to pay close attention. The sentence juxtaposes two distinct temporalities and two slightly different responses. In one, Esther "clearly" derives that her mother did not abandon her; in the other, she states that this information was consoling to her "then." Without stating exactly what her response is "now" in the time of writing, she implies that it differs from what it was initially. The alert or perhaps suspicious reader may conclude that Esther Woodcourt has revised her opinion about what once was "clear" to her younger self.

Consider also the strange comment that Esther adds after she finishes summarizing the contents of the letter. "What more the letter told me, needs not to be repeated here. It has its own times and places in my story" (583). Readers of this passage, whose importance is suggested by its being set off in a paragraph of its own, have sometimes been puzzled by Esther's failure to make good on her apparent promise to say more about the letter at a later point in her narrative. Instead, these readers note, Esther burns the letter and never mentions it again. Such readings of the paragraph are mistaken, I believe. Here, perhaps more directly than anywhere else in her narrative, Esther reveals not so much the content of her revised understanding of her mother's letter as the process by which that revised understanding makes itself known both to her and to the reader.

Notice Esther's use of the trope of prosopopoeia. It is not Lady Dedlock who tells Esther "more," but the letter itself that speaks and that presumably tells a different story from the one that Lady Dedlock wants Esther to believe. Notice also Esther's emphasis on repetition as well as her use of the small spatiotemporal adverb "here." What "more" the letter "told" her may indeed "need" to be "repeated," but not "here," not at this point in her narrative. Instead, "it has its own times and places in my story." The times and places where the unspecified "more" is repeated are scattered across the entire narrative. They speak through Esther in the form of flashbacks, unbidden recurring memories, and other uncanny repetitions. They emanate largely from Esther's unconscious, and they are the signs, the symptoms, of the unclaimed experience that shapes so much of her narrative.[11] What stands out in this passage is Esther's greater than usual awareness that there are things she somehow "knows" but cannot say and that these things have a life and temporality not entirely under her control, their "own times and places in my story."

One further example—perhaps conscious, perhaps not—of the intrusion of a memory from her earliest infancy into Esther's account of her mother's letter deserves mention. Esther summarizes the central message of Lady Dedlock's letter thus: "Her elder and only sister, the godmother of my childhood, discovering signs of life in me when I had been laid aside as dead, had, in her stern sense of duty, with no desire or willingness that I should live, reared me in rigid secrecy, and had never again beheld my mother's face from within a few hours of my birth" (583). Although perfectly grammatical, this rather lengthy complex sentence contains an odd shift in focalization toward the end that betrays its narrator's special preoccupation. The sentence has one grammatical subject, "Her . . . sister," that governs two past-perfect verbs: "had . . . reared" and "had never again beheld." The two verbs, however, are separated by intervening prepositional phrases and distanced from their grammatical subject by an apposition and a participial clause, with the result that the connection between the subject and especially the second of the two verbs is attenuated. The weakening of this connection, combined with the substitution of "my mother's face" for the expected and more consistent "her sister's face," locates this perception, not within Lady Dedlock's discourse, but within Esther's. There is no particular reason for Lady Dedlock to emphasize the fact that the godmother had not seen her sister's face "from within a few hours of [Esther's] birth," but there is every reason for Esther to do so. The shift in focalization revises Lady Dedlock's explanation and turns it into an oblique observation by Esther on her loss of connection to her mother's face while still a newborn infant. By the end of the sentence, we are no longer with the godmother, but at the scene of "my birth." Once again, the trauma of early maternal loss insists on speaking, perhaps unconsciously, through the language of Esther Woodcourt.

In focusing on the conflicted subjectivity of Esther's narrative, I do not mean to disregard entirely the ways in which she functions objectively as a force for good in the social world of the novel. Many critics have found in her a principle of coherence sufficient to offset the tendency toward drift and anomie depicted in the other narrative.[12] With her commitments to duty and responsibility and her belief in a beneficent providence, she embodies the conservative Victorian values that derive from and exert their authority over the domestic sphere. Moreover, through her actions she represents a force of charity that is conspicuously missing elsewhere in the world of the novel. Certainly, wherever she goes, she displays remarkable managerial abilities. Restoring order to broken or chaotic households is one of her chief roles in the book, and to a considerable extent she manages the task of narrator in a similarly quiet and orderly fashion.

For the most part, however, I tend to view this "Good Esther," as Dever calls her, as a defensive mask, a false self constructed in order to make up for the early deficits in her life. "I often thought," Esther writes of her experience at Greenleaf school, "of the resolution I had made on my birthday, to try to be industrious, contented, and true-hearted, and to do some good to some one, and win some love if I could" (39). The fact that Esther made this resolution on her birthday links it directly to the events surrounding her birth. Her resolution is meant as an act of reparation. Abandoned almost immediately by her biological mother (however we understand the circumstances of this action) and blighted by an emotionally punitive godmother (secretly her aunt), Esther compensates for these early injuries by becoming a mother to every abandoned or neglected child she meets, doing for them what she wishes a mother had done for her. Caddy, Ada, Richard, Charley, Jo, the little Jellybys and Pardiggles, all at some time or another come under her maternal care. It is no accident, I would suggest, that practically the first good deed she performs after arriving in London is to help release a child named Peepy by pulling his head forward through the area railing in a comic reenactment of successful parturition. Here and throughout the novel, Dickens carefully orchestrates Esther's actions and language in ways that allow her to reveal, and us to see, unconscious dimensions of her character.

Although she successfully mothers many of the other characters in the book, Esther can never make up for the absence of attentive mothering in her own life. She can never be a mother to herself. The false, dutiful, accommodating identity that she develops in order to win approval from others can be detected in the voice of self-abasement that she often adopts both as character and as narrator and that many readers have found irritatingly coy and insincere. With its frequent use of dashes, parenthetical remarks, broken syntax, reflexive verbs, and third-person self-address, Esther's rhetoric of "confusion" mirrors her frequent inner state of abjection.[13] In addition, such language often serves strategically to keep her ignorant of things she prefers not to know. At other times, her rhetoric of confusion appears to solicit contradiction. When she says that she is "not clever" or "not good" or "do[es] not know" something, not only is the reverse often objectively the case, but the form and context of her statement seem to demand disconfirmation. Whatever its motives, and they are complex, Esther's voice of confusion contrasts sharply with the powerful voice she commands at moments like the end of chapter 59. To understand Esther in the full complexity of her being requires a careful tracking of the modulations in her voice, both what she reports herself and other characters as saying and the ways in which she conducts her retrospective narration.

In addition to a false voice, Esther hides behind a set of false names: Old Woman, Cobweb, Mother Hubbard, Dame Durden, and the rest. As critics have long since pointed out, these fairytale names with their associations of old age and dirt (but also of maternity) transform Esther prematurely into an aged crone or little old woman, concealing the youth, beauty, and sexuality she is hesitant to claim—attributes suggestive of the biblical beauty queen whose name she shares. Her readiness to accept these derogatory nicknames and to allow her own name to be lost among them signals the instability of her identity and her complicity with the well-intentioned but demeaning constructions of her friends.

A name that needs to be added to this list of false identities but that has received less attention than the others is Summerson. This is the name presumably given to her by the godmother soon after Esther's birth as a means of concealing her origins and avoiding any incriminating connection to her parents. Like "Nemo," it is a name that obscures paternity, but one whose final syllable retains the trace of filiation. Viewed from a different angle, however, and with an eye alert to the complexity of Dickens's naming practices, the false name chosen by the godmother points to a deeper truth about Esther's parentage. Instead of "Summer's son," suggesting a preferred child warmed by parental love, an antithetical reading of her name gives us "Winter's daughter." Esther is and always has been the daughter of the frozen mother: "It was my mother cold and dead."[14]

As narrator, Esther would rather tell the story of other people than think or talk about herself. Eventually, and with considerable reluctance, she acknowledges that "if these pages contain a great deal about me, I can only suppose it must be because I have really something to do with them, and can't be kept out" (137). Nevertheless, she remains most comfortable when she can allow "my little body . . . [to] fall into the back-ground" (40) so that the focus falls on someone else. Falling, or pushing herself, into the background is her favorite means of narrative concealment, the textual equivalent of the burial that she gives her doll. Yet, despite her efforts to remain hidden from the reader and from herself, Esther cannot keep her unconscious from speaking. She becomes so caught up at times in the story she is telling that she allows her "body" to speak for her. It is in these moments of bodily excess, registered in different ways within the text but primarily through shifts in voice, that we can glimpse or overhear aspects of Esther—desire, anger, despair—that otherwise lie out of sight. The key to reading Esther Woodcourt, then, is her voice, and the key to understanding her voice is to trace its relation to the figure of the absent mother that she relentlessly pursues through the pages of her text, only to find her again and again "cold and dead."[15]

As an example of how such a voice-oriented reading might proceed, the passage describing Esther's departure from Windsor in chapter 3 is worth considering in some detail, for it displays many of the stylistic features that characterize her narrative discourse.

> Mrs. Rachael was too good to feel any emotion at parting, but I was not so good, and wept bitterly. I thought that I ought to have known her better after so many years, and ought to have made myself enough of a favorite with her to make her sorry then. When she gave me one cold parting kiss upon my forehead, like a thaw-drop from the stone porch—it was a very frosty day—I felt so miserable and self-reproachful, that I clung to her and told her it was my fault, I knew, that she could say good-bye so easily!
> "No, Esther!" she returned. "It is your misfortune!" (35–36)

What strikes most readers immediately as odd about this passage is its misalignment of affect and judgment. Esther praises Mrs. Rachael for her lack of emotion at the moment of parting and blames herself for not having done more to earn the older woman's affection. In this bizarre reversal of attributions, we recognize Esther's all too familiar tendency toward self-abasement along with an implicit and perhaps irritatingly manipulative—because indirect—demand for reassurance. "No, Esther, it's not your fault," we are tempted to say, "but I wish you didn't always put me in the position of having to say so."[16]

A voice-oriented reading of this exchange, one that focuses on what Esther is doing as narrator, would view it somewhat differently. In addition to acknowledging the symptomatic and manipulative qualities of her language, such a reading would give the adult Esther more credit for understanding both Mrs. Rachael's cruel withholding of affection and her own excessive (and neurotic) self-reproach. Narrating the episode of departure allows the older Esther to reexperience the feelings she had as a girl, and to begin putting them behind her. It also allows her to represent the experience in such a way as to leave the reader in no doubt about where praise and blame properly belong. Both a manipulative plea for reassurance and a tentative step toward self-understanding, the passage is at the same time a clear-sighted if oblique criticism directed at an older woman who caused Esther needless emotional pain.

But it is much else besides. Esther's comparison of Mrs. Rachael's parting kiss to "a thaw-drop from the stone porch" links this moment in the text to the Ghost's Walk refrain, "drip, drip, drip," already sounded by the other narrator in chapter 2. Figurative language is relatively infrequent in Esther's discourse, and when a striking example such as this one appears, some readers have seen it as evidence that Dickens, not Esther, is doing the writing. Rather than take Esther's striking simile as conventional foreshadowing, however, or as an intrusion by Dickens into Esther's text, a voice-oriented reading would consider it a retroactive trace—literally an echo—of Esther's own ghostwalking experience in chapter 36, after the failed reunion scene, and of her association of the Ghost's Walk with the submerged story of her origins that she repeatedly attempts to recover in writing about other moments in her life.

The grief and loss that she reports experiencing upon leaving Windsor seem vastly out of proportion to what we know about her relationship with Mrs. Rachael. The godmother's only servant, Mrs. Rachael is described by Esther as "another very good woman, but austere to me" (29). A few pages later, Esther reports feeling grateful "towards Mrs. Rachael, who was a widow; and O, towards her daughter, of whom she was proud, who came to see her once a fortnight!" (31). The "O" interjected prior to mentioning the daughter is our clue to the residue of pain that Esther feels, even in the time of writing, at the thought of a cherished mother-daughter bond of the kind she can never have.

In writing the scene of separation from Mrs. Rachael, Esther as narrator is thus reworking a series of other cold farewell scenes from her past that stretch back to the unnarrated moment of her birth and forward, narratively speaking, to the discovery of her mother's body. The echoes in this passage of the scene of Lady Dedlock's death are especially strong. Esther begins her description of the departure from Windsor by announcing the arrival of the coach that will carry her to Greenleaf school:

> The coach was at the little lawn gate—we had not come out until we heard the wheels—and thus I left her, with a sorrowful heart. She went in before my boxes were lifted to the coach-roof, and shut the door. As long as I could see the house, I looked back at it from the window, through my tears. My godmother had left Mrs. Rachael all the little property she possessed; and there was to be a sale; and an old hearth-rug with roses on it, which always seemed to me the first thing in the world I had ever seen, was hanging outside in the frost and snow. (36)

Among the many associations to the scene of Lady Dedlock's death are details like the "little lawn-gate," which recalls the "iron gate" of the graveyard in which Hawdon/Nemo is buried and where Lady Dedlock dies. Likewise, the sound of the wheels that brings Esther out of the house is an auditory memory of the churning wheels of Bucket's coach during the chase sequence. (Notice, again, the importance of Esther's self-interruptions and of information contained in statements set off by dashes.) Most powerful of all, however, is the description of the hearth rug hanging outside in the frost and snow, a memory trace of the mother's dead body—and specifically of her face—as it is revealed at the end of chapter 59; but also the trace of Esther's earliest childhood memory, an image of the mother's face (or perhaps her breast) recalled from infancy: "the first thing in the world I had ever seen." The roses on the hearth rug are like the "beautiful complexion and rosy lips" (27) of Esther's doll, the doll that she describes burying before she leaves Windsor for the school, and which in turn are a reflection of Esther's own features. The hearth rug is thus one of Esther's many mirrors in the book, one connected both with death and with the mother's face. In leaving the hearth rug behind and in writing about it as she does, Esther thus repeats her mother's abandonment of her as well as her own experience of leaving behind the dead body of her mother.

The most difficult and painful part of these condensed and displaced memory fragments for Esther is the fear, even as she writes about them in the present, that somehow she was and is responsible for her mother's rejection of her. Daughterly desire for the mother's love, daughterly anger at the mother's abandonment—both give way to the nagging question, is it my fault that she could say goodbye so easily? The profound and undeniable truth that comes back to her in the voice of Mrs. Rachael is "No, Esther! . . . It is your misfortune." Whether these are words actually spoken by Mrs. Rachael, or whether these are Esther's own words projected and received back by her, is a question that even a voice-oriented reading cannot presume to resolve.

In a voice-oriented reading, every voice belongs potentially to the narrator. The question, who speaks? becomes impossible to answer with certainty, since in the discourse every character speaks only at the pleasure and direction of the one who controls that discourse. Every character is thus potentially a ventriloquist's dummy (or doll), and every narrator potentially a Little Swills, the comic vocalist who re-creates the inquest for customers at the Sol's Arms by taking every part and performing each in turn.

To imagine Esther as a comic vocalist, projecting voices onto other characters, may take some adjustment in our thinking, but it proves a useful way of understanding certain passages in the novel where speech attribution and address remain ambiguous. Consider, for example, the crucial scene in chapter 8 where Esther reports observing the death of the brickmaker's baby. Dever is correct in calling this a "primal scene" in which Esther phantasmatically witnesses the moment of her death in infancy.[17] Not surprisingly, Esther is the first to notice what happens, and she reports what she sees with a simple, unadorned statement—"The child died" (134)—whose very brevity betrays the emotional impact we presume this scene to have had upon her. And yet, while Ada and the other woman in the cottage dissolve in tears, we look in vain for any sign of Esther's reaction, either at the time of the event or in the moment of re-experiencing it. Instead of telling us what she felt then or feels now, Esther describes how she went about her domestic duties, laying the baby's body on a shelf, covering it with her handkerchief, and comforting the mother.

A reading of the scene that attends more closely to voice and to the possibility of vocal displacement need not look far for Esther's reaction. "'O Esther!' cried Ada sinking on her knees beside it. 'Look here! O Esther, my love, the little thing! The suffering, quiet, pretty little thing! I am so sorry for it. I am so sorry for the mother. I never saw a sight so pitiful as this before! O baby, baby!'" (134). Esther projects her own feelings about the baby's death onto Ada and expresses them through the voice of the Ada character. It is not enough to speak of Ada here as Esther's alter ego or double. While this is certainly true, it elides Esther's agency as narrator in controlling the representation and voicing. A more detailed reading of the entire passage would note how she carefully fuses herself and Ada into the pronoun "we" at the beginning of the scene, then splits the two apart into an "I" and "she" in order to present the unvoiced and voiced portions of her reaction, and then closes the gap again with the undifferentiated pronoun "we."

A voice-sensitive reading of this passage allows for other possibilities as well. If we accept Dever's contention that in this scene Esther is re-experiencing phantasmatically the trauma of her birth/death, then all four women present in the scene—the two brickmakers' wives, Esther, and Ada—can be seen as aspects of a single mother imago in relation to the dead infant, who occupies the place of Esther. Understood in this fashion, the women's collective response of grief, devotion, and mutual concern stands in sharp contrast to the alternate fantasy of cold rejection that Esther retains and projects on other occasions, for instance in her account of leaving Windsor. In such a reading, Ada's reaction holds special interest, for in it Esther as narrator allows herself to entertain the fantasy of a loving mother overcome with grief at the loss of a cherished newborn child. Ada's grief-stricken cry, "O Esther! . . . O Esther, my love, the little thing!" thus resounds with a different meaning and has a different addressee. It is the cry that Esther wishes her mother could have addressed to her on that fateful occasion, instead of the cold rebuff that she imagines in its place and that she has actually experienced under different circumstances in the reunion scene of chapter 36.

Esther's commentary immediately following Ada's reaction exposes another rhetorical layer of this scene and another, again phantasmatic, addressee for Esther's narrative performance. "Such compassion," she writes, describing Ada, "such gentleness, as that with which she bent down weeping, and put her hand upon the mother's, might have softened any mother's heart that ever beat" (134). The fantasy here is that Ada's gesture of tenderness—and Esther's narrative re-creation of it—might soften the heart not just of "any mother," but of one mother in particular. If we ask who is the addressee of the entire narrative that Esther writes, who is "the unknown friend to whom I write," as she puts it in her final chapter, one answer has to be that it is "my mother cold and dead."

Another important scene to which any voice-oriented reading of *Bleak House* must pay close attention is Esther's report in chapter 18 of the encounter between Lady Dedlock and herself in the keeper's lodge during a thunderstorm.[18] Esther has already had the experience of seeing Lady Dedlock in church and of finding her face like "a broken glass . . . , in which I saw scraps of old remembrances" (292). The following Saturday, while walking in the woods near Chesney Wold, she, Ada, and Jarndyce are overtaken by a sudden storm and seek refuge in a little keeper's lodge. As the two young women sit, just within the doorway, to watch the storm, a voice speaks.

> "Is it not dangerous to sit in so exposed a place?"
> "O no, Esther dear!" said Ada, quietly.
> Ada said it to me; but, *I* had not spoken.
> The beating at my heart came back again. I had never heard the voice, as I had never seen the face, but it affected me in the same strange way. Again, in a moment, there arose before my mind innumerable pictures of myself. (296)

The voice is of course Lady Dedlock's, and Esther's response, as in the church, is to be flooded with confused remembrances of herself and her past. It is a voice that she says she had never heard, yet one that sounds strangely familiar, a voice so much like her own that even Ada mistakes the source. What are we to make of this uncanny confusion of tongues, and what is Esther doing with it in her narration?

The first thing to point out is the highly ambiguous nature of Lady Dedlock's question. Dangerous to whom? Ostensibly an innocent and well-meaning expression of concern about the two young women's exposure to the weather, the question also lends itself to a darker interpretation. The danger could be just as much if not more to Lady Dedlock, and the exposure not that of sitting near the door of the lodge, but of Esther's appearing in any public place where her resemblance to her mother could endanger that lady's high social position. "Is it not dangerous [to me] [for you] to sit in so exposed a place?" If this is the meaning that hovers beneath the surface of her courteous concern, then its implications for Esther are dire. It signals, from the moment of their first speaking, Lady Dedlock's barely concealed wish that Esther should not be seen, should disappear, should die. I do not mean to claim that this is what Lady Dedlock actually intends, consciously or unconsciously. We do not have access to her inner thoughts. But I do think it is what Esther hears and remembers her mother saying. At the time, Esther does not appear to recognize this darker meaning in Lady Dedlock's words, but can we be so sure? I am inclined to hypothesize a silent, watchful, and suspicious Esther, a Hortense if you will, who accompanies Lady Dedlock and examines her every word and movement for signs of selfishness and aversion to her daughter. I believe it is this Esther who narrates the scene, who puts the ambiguous question in Lady Dedlock's mouth, and who lets its more sinister implication color her account of the remainder of their meeting.

But what if Ada is correct? What if Esther is the one who said these words? Or what if Esther, in repeating them in her narrative, has allowed the ambiguity of speaker to linger, so that she and we can read them as her own? Reformulated along these lines, the sentence would read: "Is it not dangerous [to my mother] [for me] to sit in so exposed a place?" Such a reading would place the recognition of dangerous exposure within Esther herself and would lead, as I shall argue shortly, to the hypothesis that Esther's illness, and especially her disfigurement, are the result not merely of contact with a contagious disease but also of Esther's unconscious wish to protect her mother by effacing the physical resemblance between them. "Exposure" and "danger" are the terms on which the entire interaction pivots. Esther exposes herself to the danger of disease so that her mother can avoid exposure to danger of a different kind.

After some further conversation between Lady Dedlock and Jarndyce, during which Esther remains silent but focuses closely on what she describes as Lady Dedlock's "indifferent manner" (297), the scene concludes with Esther's account of the curious episode involving Lady Dedlock and her two attendants. Although Esther does not speak, her narrative reconstruction of the event and of Hortense's strange departure, walking barefoot through the grass, contains more direct traces of the anger she still harbors toward her mother than any other portion of the book.

As Esther presents it, the altercation between Lady Dedlock and Hortense takes the by now familiar form of a mother's rejection of an unwanted daughter. Only this time, the pain of maternal rejection is compounded by the presence of a desired daughter, Rosa.

> "I am your maid, my Lady, at the present," said the Frenchwoman. "The message was for the attendant."
>
> "I was afraid you might mean me, my Lady," said the pretty girl.
>
> "I did mean you, child," replied her mistress, calmly. (299)

Esther then reports Lady Dedlock's polite words of farewell, in which, although they are addressed to Mr. Jarndyce, she clearly infers—as the phrase set off in dashes indicates—the mother's wish never again to see her rejected child.

> "I am sorry," said Lady Dedlock to Mr. Jarndyce, "that we are not likely to resume our former acquaintance. You will allow me to send the carriage back for your two wards. It shall be here directly."
>
> But, as he would on no account accept this offer, she took a graceful leave of Ada—none of me—and put her hand upon his proffered arm, and got into the carriage; which was a little, low, park carriage, with a hood.

> "Come in, child!" she said to the pretty girl, "I shall want you. Go on!"
>
> The carriage rolled away; and the Frenchwoman, with the wrappers she had brought hanging over her arm, remained standing where she had alighted.
>
> I suppose there is nothing Pride can so little bear with, as Pride itself, and that she was punished for her imperious manner. Her retaliation was the most singular I could have imagined. She remained perfectly still until the carriage had turned into the drive, and then, without the least discomposure of countenance, slipped off her shoes, left them on the ground, and walked deliberately in the same direction, through the wettest of the wet grass. (299)

Despite her steadfast silence, we have no difficulty imagining what Esther is feeling here. The Esther who narrates this scene has taken great care to notice and record every imagined slight, every use of the word "child" to someone other than herself, every sign of what she takes as Lady Dedlock's "displeasure or dislike" (298). Rather than acknowledge openly the hurt and anger she then felt, and still feels, at her mother's preference for what she repeatedly calls "the pretty girl," Esther displaces her own reaction onto Hortense, just as she did onto Ada in the scene with the dead baby.

Whereas in the earlier scene Esther reveals herself by means of a dislocated voice, here displacement takes the form of action. The ventriloquist's doll not only speaks, it moves. It moves, however, only by virtue of and through the language of the narrator who gives it life. Hortense's transgressive action finds expression through Esther's retrospective voice. Consider the extraordinary sentence describing Hortense's return to Chesney Wold with which Esther brings the chapter to a close: "Still, very steadfastly and quietly walking towards it, a peaceful figure too in the landscape, went Mademoiselle Hortense, shoeless, through the wet grass" (300). There is no "confusion" here on Esther's part, only an exquisite and carefully controlled rage. The elegant inversion of subject and verb, the semantic and temporal ambiguity of the initial "Still," combining motion and stasis and pulling the completed action of the past-tense verb "went" back into the timeless present of writing—all this bespeaks a superb control of language. As this sentence demonstrates, Esther can be a powerful prose stylist when her deepest feelings, in this case anger, are engaged.

The closest Esther comes in this passage to voicing her anger directly is the curious moral speculation she offers as the Dedlock carriage rolls away. "I suppose," she writes, "there is nothing Pride can so little bear with, as Pride itself, and that she was punished for her imperious manner." The general context and the sentence that immediately follows restrict this sentiment to Hortense, but the ambiguity of pronoun reference, together with the sentence's position at the beginning of a new paragraph (a change introduced late in Dickens's process of revision), allows the accusation of Pride to apply to Lady Dedlock and the speculation regarding "punishment" to suggest, ever so faintly, Esther's grim satisfaction that in her exposure, and ultimately in her death, the cold mother may receive—indeed has already received (the verb is a simple past tense)—just what she deserves.

Closer attention to questions of voice and temporality may also shed light on one of the most puzzling passages in the book and on an aspect of the mysterious illness that befalls Esther halfway through the novel. Chapter 31, "Nurse and Patient," is the exact midpoint of the novel, the middle chapter of monthly number 10, itself the middle number of the nineteen-part serialization. The passage from this centrally positioned chapter that I want to analyze in detail is introduced by a paragraph of chiaroscuro landscape description, full of gothic elements and written in a style untypical of Esther—untypical, that is, of the domestic busybody persona that she often adopts, but more typical, I would argue, of the darker, more complex writing self that emerges whenever her narrative approaches the topic of her mother and begins to draw on the resources of her unconscious mind. "Towards London," she writes, "a lurid glare overhung the whole dark waste; and the contrast between these two lights, and the fancy which the redder light engendered of an unearthly fire, gleaming on all the unseen buildings of the city, and on all the faces of its many thousands of wondering inhabitants, was as solemn as might be" (488). Passages like these, with their darker content, complex syntax, and use of figurative language, often function as preludes to a ghostly encounter of some sort.

The next paragraph reads as follows:

> I had no thought, that night—none, I am quite sure—of what was soon to happen to me. But I have always remembered since, that when we had stopped at the garden gate to look up at the sky, and when we went upon our way, I had for a moment an undefinable impression of myself as being something different from what I then was. I know it was then, and there, that I had it. I have ever since connected the feeling with that spot and time, and with everything associated with that spot and time, to the distant voices in the town, the barking of a dog, and the sound of wheels coming down the miry hill. (489)

Several critics have noticed this passage, but none has been able to identify or explain the strange experience it describes.[19] By now we should be able to recognize this as another of Esther's temporally complex, uncanny moments. Tonally and even in content, it resembles some of Esther's descriptions of visiting Chesney Wold and walking on the Ghost's Walk. The passage mixes verb tenses (simple past, past perfect, present perfect, present), a confusing surplus of temporal markers (that night; soon; always; since then; then, and there; ever since; that spot and time), associated contemporary sounds (voices, a barking dog, the sound of wheels), and vague pronoun reference (who are "I," "me," and "myself"? how do we understand the word "something"? to what does "it" refer?) to describe with vivid particularity an experience identified only as "an undefinable impression of myself as being something different from what I then was."

Psychoanalyst Christopher Bollas has a useful term for the kind of knowledge Esther describes here. He calls it "the unthought known."[20] Such knowledge, according to Bollas, is preverbal and extra-rational, but it is no less certain or real. It is a knowledge held in the body or in the unconscious or preconscious mind. It resembles the knowledge acquired in infancy, such as the smell or taste of the mother, the sound of her voice, the distant memory of her face—the entire relational matrix between mother and baby. Esther insists that she knew something, but without thinking. She had "no thought, that night—none I am quite sure"—but in that moment, she knew herself to be "different" in some way that defies explanation.

Critics have suggested that "what was soon to happen to me" refers proleptically to the disease that Esther will contract by the end of the chapter, but this explanation, while satisfactory as far as it goes, seems insufficient to me. The clause, with its vague temporal adverb "soon," can refer equally and more immediately to the uncanny experience described in the rest of the paragraph. My own suggestion is that Esther saw or sensed the presence of a ghost and that in writing about it she re-creates and reenters that disorienting, hallucinatory encounter. I think the ghost is Lady Dedlock and that in this paragraph Esther is describing the moment when she came to the sudden "unthought" realization of who her mother was and is.

What about the auditory memories, the barking dog and other sounds that Esther reports associating with this experience? On the one hand, they help her to pinpoint the exact time and place where she had the undefinable impression of her difference, and as such they add to the particularity and realism of her account. On the other hand, precisely because they are auditory and nonverbal and are filtered through the retrospective, potentially inexact memory of the older Esther, they partake of the "unthought known." The temporal location of sound is often difficult to specify. It is possible, then, that Esther may be confusing or conflating two different experiences of voices and barking dogs, one from chapter 36, where she reports hearing "deep voices" (584) and "the barking of the dogs" (586) while walking on the grounds of Chesney Wold, and the other in the uncanny passage from chapter 31. Both sets of sounds, of course, recall ghostly near encounters with her mother. Similarly, "the sound of wheels coming down the miry hill" in chapter 31 echoes—at the same time that it anticipates discursively—Esther's recollection of the "miry sleet" (885) through which Bucket's coach "churned—with a sound as if it were a beach of small shells—under the hoofs of the horses, into mire and water" (880)—another passage closely linked to Esther's desire for reconnection with the mother. The fact that these auditory details appear later in Esther's narrative does not prevent them from inflecting her description of the experience in chapter 31, since those events and sounds have already occurred to her in life prior to their narrativization in Esther's written account. Once again, *sjužet* repeats *fabula,* creating the potential for "echoes" in the text of as yet unnarrated material.

If I am correct in suggesting that Esther already "knew" who her mother was prior to contracting the disease, this possibility has implications for other parts of the plot. We know that Esther fell ill after being exposed to Charley and that Charley acquired the disease from Jo. An important difference between Esther's and Charley's experience of the disease, however, is that Esther was disfigured, her face scarred beyond recognition, whereas Charley was not. Individuals of course have different immune systems and respond differently to contagious diseases. Notice, however, that the disease is never named. Critics have argued about what the disease might be, with most settling for smallpox, but a few proposing erysipelas.[21] In the text, the only term used for the disease is "fever." I believe that it is a mistake to insist on treating Dickens as entirely a realist on this point. The disease is certainly real enough in one sense; Jo dies of it. But it is also a gothic device or, what amounts to the same thing, a psychogenic force.

Lady Dedlock does not reveal herself to be Esther's mother until after Esther has recovered from her illness. But if Esther "knew" in some fashion, before being exposed to Charley, who her mother is and what the social consequences to Lady Dedlock of revealing this information to the world would be, then it is possible that Esther, in some unthinking or unconscious way, purposely exposed herself to the "fever" and then, having contracted it, made use of the disease in order to protect her mother by eliminating the facial resemblance between them. I am suggesting, in other words, that Dickens makes Esther's illness, and specifically her disfigurement, the result of a pathological accommodation on her part to what she takes as her mother's deepest wish—that she should, if not exactly die, at least destroy the incriminating evidence written on her face. Disfigurement and the blank depression that underlies the forced cheer and dutiful obedience of Esther's public persona—and that continue to afflict the older Esther even as she writes her account of these events—are thus the daughter's way of maintaining an unconscious identification with her "dead mother."[22]

It is of course impossible to prove such a hypothesis, but the hypothesis does have the virtue of offering a plausible explanation for Esther's uncanny experience of "difference" from herself in chapter 31. Moreover, it is consistent with the relief that Esther reports having immediately upon learning from Lady Dedlock that she is Esther's mother: the "burst of gratitude to the providence of God that I was so changed as that I never could disgrace her by any trace of likeness; as that nobody could ever now look at me, and look at her, and remotely think of any near tie between us" (579). What Esther here calls her "burst" of gratitude I take to be the bursting into consciousness at this later time of the life-altering recognition and experience of difference from herself, resulting ultimately in a wish for self-effacement, that first flashed upon her unconsciously in the scene she describes in chapter 31.[23]

2
ILLUSTRATION

PERHAPS THE MOST STARTLING REALIZATION TO EMERGE IN connection with the foregoing reflections on voice and temporality in *Bleak House* has been the extent to which these issues permeate the novel's illustrations. At the risk of taking what may at first seem like a detour from my primary emphasis on Esther Woodcourt, I want to ask a simple question: who narrates the illustrations in *Bleak House?* To put the question in these terms presupposes, of course, that the illustrations are narratives. Without attempting to argue this claim, I want to suspend the question for now and approach it from a slightly different angle.

Bleak House is famously a novel with two narrators. It is also a novel illustrated by Dickens's collaborator, Hablot K. Browne ("Phiz"). Inevitably, the question arises of how to understand the connection between the illustrations and the two narrators. The illustrations are by Phiz. They belong to him. His vision, sometimes influenced by requests or suggestions from Dickens, shapes and determines the images that we see on the page. Phiz's control of technique, his knowledge of artistic convention and tradition (iconography, emblem, composition, and so on), are responsible for the visual forms before us. He, together with Dickens, is the author to whom we might reasonably refer in making inferences about the source, intention, and meaning of these works of art.[1]

At the same time that they belong to Dickens and Phiz, however, the illustrations "belong" in another sense to the two narrators. Each plate accompanies and illustrates a passage in the text narrated by one of them. Should we then assume that the illustrations that accompany passages presented by the general narrator are "narrated" by "him" and that those that accompany passages told by Esther are "narrated" by her? Fortunately, the situation is not so simple. Moreover, as if things were not already complicated enough, what are we to make of the fact that the *Bleak House* illustrations exhibit two distinct graphic styles: the linear, caricatural, often emblematic style familiar from Phiz's illustrations to previous Dickens novels and the more "painterly," atmospheric style of the novel's so-calleddark plates? Do these two styles correspond in some way to the novel's two narrators or perhaps to Esther's two personas: the "Good Esther," as Dever and I like to call her, and the other, darker self that emerges in connection with memories of her mother? Once again, the situation is more complicated than such simple equations would allow.

Let me attempt to put some order into these speculations. First, I propose that we abandon for all practical purposes the notion of Dickens/Phiz as the controlling consciousness responsible for the illustrations. Appeals to the authority of the "author," though not entirely irrelevant to the understanding of a work of art, whether verbal or visual, are needlessly restrictive. In place of the author, I propose substituting the narratological concept of focalization, especially as developed by theorist Mieke Bal first with respect to verbal narratives and subsequently with respect to visual images.[2] As applied to visual narratives, the concept of focalization presumes that every image is seen from some particular aspect or aspects. Revising the framework initially proposed by Genette for verbal narratives only, Bal proposes a flexible and dynamic schema in which the interaction of different perspectives often constitutes one of the principal subjects of an image, whatever other "content" it may have. In Bal's schema, there are two principal kinds of focalization: external and character-based. Influenced to a considerable extent by Benveniste's theories of subjectivity in language, Bal's model also devotes considerable attention to the ways in which images address their viewer or beholder.[3]

If we begin to think of the illustrations to *Bleak House* in relation to Bal's model of focalization, several promising possibilities emerge. In the first place, all of the illustrations may be considered as externally focalized—that is, as seen by a viewer who stands outside the depicted scene and who is not a character in the novel. This viewpoint is roughly analogous though not identical to the perspective of the unnamed present-tense narrator in the verbal text. We might call this the viewpoint of a "heteroperceptive" focalizer, by analogy with Genette's concept of the heterodiegetic narrator of a verbal text. Within each illustration, however, there are often multiple lines of sight that call attention to internal, character-based focalizations. Usually these internal focalizers are actual characters whom we recognize from the text, but sometimes they are inanimate or nonhuman figures: pictures on the wall, for example, or other curiously sighted figures. A good example of this latter kind is the doll hanging in the background at the top of "The appointed time," the illustration that depicts Guppy's arrival on the scene of Krook's spontaneous combustion (fig. 1). Another example in the same image is the cat, Lady Jane, whose eyes seem to focus on the spot from which Krook has disappeared and that Guppy and Weevle have not yet identified.

Drawing attention to these internal focalizers in the illustrations can remind us of how often characters (and even objects) in the verbal narrative scrutinize each other and remain "on the watch." Tulkinghorn and Hortense are particularly intense watchers. Guppy is their comic counterpart. Esther too is a watcher, as she admits somewhat reluctantly near the beginning of her narrative. "I had always rather a noticing way—not a quick way, O no!—a silent way of noticing what passed before me, and thinking I should like to understand it better" (28). A notable example of inanimate watching in the text is the pair of "gaunt holes" (164), pierced in the shutters of Nemo's room, that keep watch over the dead law writer's corpse through the still hours of the night in chapter 11. Similarly, long rows of houses in the vicinity of Lady Dedlock's London mansion "stare at each other with that severity, that half a dozen of its greatest mansions seem to have been slowly stared into stone, rather than originally built in that material" (738). Even London's old oil street lamps, now replaced by new gas fixtures, retain

FIG. 1. "The appointed time."

strange powers of sight: "Even oil itself, yet lingering at long intervals in a little absurd glass pot, with a knob in the bottom like an oyster, blinks and sulks at newer lights every night, like its high and dry master in the House of Lords" (738).

Many of the *Bleak House* illustrations take seeing and not seeing as their subject and exploit the possibilities of internal, character-based focalization. "Mr. Guppy's desolation," for example, shows a rapt audience staring at an unseen theatrical performance outside the image to the viewer's right (fig. 2). Presumably the play is a comedy, since everyone is smiling. Meanwhile, a disconsolate Guppy, standing at the left of the scene, gazes up forlornly from the pit to where Esther, seated with

Ada, Richard, and Jarndyce, tries unsuccessfully to avoid looking back at him. The comedy of Esther's embarrassment as reported in her text—she enjoys Guppy's admiration and at the same time wants to discourage it—is repeated in the illustration, with its multiple lines of sight. Guppy is not alone, moreover, in his erotic gazing. Doubling Esther's comic-pathetic lover, Richard peers down at Ada rather than at the play.

Another, more complex exploration of sightlines and character-based focalization is "The little church in the park," the illustration that

FIG. 2. "Mr. Guppy's desolation."

corresponds to Esther's description in chapter 18 of first seeing Lady Dedlock at church (fig. 3). In this image, as in "Mr. Guppy's desolation," a large group of people observes a public performance, here the religious service, while a different, more intense drama of watching goes on within the scene. From the Dedlock box on the left, Lady Dedlock stares across the nave at Esther, sitting with her friends. Esther's line of sight is more difficult to parse; she looks back in Lady Dedlock's general direction (the viewer's left), but her glance may be directed toward the servants' corner, at bottom left, where a bonneted female figure with an ambiguously smiling face ostensibly looks down at her prayer book, but may actually be watching Esther, or perhaps watching Lady Dedlock watching Esther. This presumably is Hortense (her bonnet is of a different style from the other women), who, according to Esther's text, "seemed maliciously watchful of this pretty girl [Rosa in the text, but perhaps also Esther herself], and indeed of everyone and everything there. It was a Frenchwoman's [face]" (290). The inner drama of the image lies in the interplay of character-based focalized perspectives and in the tense watching and counterwatching that goes on.

The *Bleak House* illustrations present another kind of internal, character-based focalization. Many, though not all, of the illustrations can be read as if seen from outside the image by an observer whom we know from inside the verbal text. Usually, but not always, this invisible viewpoint belongs to Esther. Of the novel's forty illustrations (including the frontispiece and vignette title page but not the cover wrapper), nineteen correspond to passages in Esther's narrative and twenty-one to passages reported by the other narrator. Of those that correspond to passages in the other, present-tense narrative, most do not suggest the presence of an invisible internal focalizer located outside the frame of the image. But there are some exceptions. Consider "Consecrated ground," for example, which shows the crossing sweeper, Jo, pointing through the iron gate into the graveyard where Nemo is buried (fig. 4). The scene occurs at the end of the guided tour of sites associated with her dead lover that Jo gives to the disguised Lady Dedlock.

The illustration presumably corresponds to the moment when Jo spots a rat and cries out excitedly, "Hi! Look! There he goes! Ho! Into the ground!" (262).[4] Jo points, and Lady Dedlock looks, but, as in "The

Appointed Time," the two excited onlookers do not see something that they could be noticing. The viewpoint of this illustration is from inside the graveyard. The unseen viewer, I suggest, is Captain Hawdon, or rather his ghost. Just a minute before, Jo had pointed out the grave where Nemo was buried, but the rat has distracted his and our attention. As if conjured up by Jo and Lady Dedlock's presence, however, the ghost of Hawdon has arisen and here looks at them, at the woman he once loved and at the boy whom he befriended and whose unforgettable refrain "He was wery good to me, he wos!" (178, 181) serves as Hawdon's epitaph.

FIG. 3. "The little church in the park."

As if in confirmation of this suggestion, the verbal text contains a passage whose ambiguous voicing hints at the ghostly presence of the dead law writer. Chapter 11, "Our Dear Brother," concludes with the following direct address:

> Jo, is it thou? Well, well! Though a rejected witness, who "can't exactly say" what will be done to him in greater hands than men's, thou art not quite in outer darkness. There is something like a distant ray of light in thy muttered reason for this:
> "He wos wery good to me, he wos!" (181)

FIG. 4. "Consecrated ground."

The voice that speaks here is that of the narrator, addressing Jo with the intimate second-person pronoun "thou," but it is also Nemo's voice, tenderly acknowledging and responding to Jo's kindness toward him in death as in life. Free indirect discourse blends the voice of ghost and heterodiegetic narrator.

By far the largest number of unseen internally focalized viewpoints in the *Bleak House* illustrations belongs to Esther. These illustrations always have a double temporality. They depict an event that happened to Esther Summerson in the past and in which a figure representing the character of Esther is usually present, but at the same time these illustrations correspond to and can be aligned with the retrospective viewpoint of Esther Woodcourt as she remembers and reexperiences these events in the time of writing. In other words, they illustrate both *fabula* and *sjužet*, both story time and discourse time. In narratological terms, they are "homoperceptive"—"narrated" or seen by someone who is also a character in the story.

Any illustration that corresponds to a passage in the verbal text narrated by Esther can serve as an example of this double temporality. The two illustrations previously considered, "Mr. Guppy's desolation" and "The little church in the park," can both be read as focalized by the retrospective Esther, who remembers these scenes and in them watches herself being the object of someone else's sight and, conversely, sees herself watching other characters. Another good example is "The Little old Lady," the illustration that accompanies Esther's description in chapter 3 of meeting Miss Flite outside the Court of Chancery (fig. 5). Esther stands at the center of the composition, her back toward the viewer and her bonneted head turned toward Miss Flite, who stands to her left. On the right are Richard and Ada, Richard in profile and Ada observed in full face. The image corresponds straightforwardly to an event from Esther's past; this is its story time. The image can also be read as focalized by the adult Esther, thus as the visual memory of an event from her past; this is its discourse time.

The principal clue to the image's retrospective focalization is the fact that Esther's face is not visible. Rather than attribute this element of the picture to Phiz and to his introduction in this, the book's first illustration, of the motif of the hidden face, I prefer to read Esther's bodily posture and averted face as indications of her desire as both narrator and retrospective focalizer to hide herself from the reader/viewer and to shift attention to other people, in this case to Miss Flite, on whom all the other characters appear to turn their eyes. Read retrospectively in this fashion, the image acquires other potential meaning. Esther here positions herself between two other female figures, one old and wizened, the other young and beautiful. Although standing slightly closer to Ada and with her lower body apparently oriented toward her "darling," as she has already begun to call her in the text, Esther twists her

FIG. 5. "The Little old Lady."

upper body and head in Miss Flite's direction.[5] This image, I suggest, is one of the novel's earliest mirror scenes. Esther here records her visual memory of turning away from a face that reflects her own youth and beauty and turning instead to a face and identity that offer a safer place for her to hide, that of "the Little old Lady." The picture's caption is thus ambiguous (whose voice speaks these captions anyway, we well may wonder?) and refers to Esther as much as or more than to Miss Flite. In its triple female representation, moreover, the illustration again recalls Jo's baffled but resonant question: "Is there *three* of 'em, then?"

ILLUSTRATION

Not all of Esther's retrospective, internally focalized images contain the figure of her younger self. Consider "The Ghost's Walk," for example, the illustration that corresponds to Esther's description in chapter 36 of walking on the grounds of Chesney Wold following the crucial reunion scene with her mother (fig. 6). The passage in the text

FIG. 6. "The Ghost's Walk."

that accompanies this illustration is one of the most powerful, syntactically complex, and imagistically vivid pieces of writing in the whole novel. Too long to quote in its entirety and too beautiful to submit to the distortive surgery of excerpting, this passage is further proof of Esther Woodcourt's masterful control of style and the gorgeous narrative voice that she commands on occasions when her mother hovers nearby and she begins to assume her ghostwriting persona. The illustration contains no human figures. The only sign of human presence is the "one lighted window that," as Esther writes, "might be my mother's" (586). Human presence, however, is very much in evidence by virtue of the fact that the scene is observed. Its double temporality lies in its record of an event from Esther's past; it is what she saw on that occasion. But it is also what she remembers now, in retrospect. The heavily shaded, atmospheric style of the image (this is the novel's first "dark plate") corresponds both to the evening setting of Esther's ghostwalking experience and to the dark, shadowy memory that this experience continues to evoke in her. Of the novel's ten dark plates, only three (and possibly a fourth, as I discuss in chapter 4) are retrospectively focalized through Esther, and all of them (the other two being "The Night" and "The Morning") center on Esther's desire to get closer to her mother. The dark style of these plates corresponds to the "dark" voice of Esther's retrospective narrative.

Chapter 36, containing Esther's report of the crucial reunion scene with Lady Dedlock, is unusual in having two illustrations devoted to scenes within it. The second illustration, already discussed, is "The Ghost's Walk." The first, "Lady Dedlock in the Wood," is perhaps the most important image in the entire novel and certainly one of the most complex in terms of voice and temporality (fig. 7). The illustration depicts the scene of reunion between Esther and her mother. Lady Dedlock rushes forward from the left, arms outstretched, face visible beneath her bonnet, her upper body leaning toward the figure of her daughter. Esther, seated on a small bench that encircles the trunk of a large, heavily foliaged tree, appears to wait calmly. Her face, now scarred from the disease, is hidden by her bonnet. We cannot tell if she has seen her mother, but her hands, slightly raised above her lap, suggest that she may have done so. Lady Dedlock's clothing and Esther's are much

ILLUSTRATION 39

FIG. 7. "Lady Dedlock in the Wood."

alike, emphasizing a similarity that lingers between them despite the scarring that has removed their facial resemblance. In the right background, her face turned away from the viewer and her figure more lightly etched than those of the two principal actors in the scene, kneels Charley. She is gathering violets, Esther tells us in her text. The handle and oval outline of a basket are visible on the ground next to her. Her bonnet and outer clothing lie on the ground beside Esther. In the distance, behind her, Chesney Wold is faintly visible.

The double temporality of this image, as with all the illustrations that correspond to passages narrated by Esther, is clear: there is the time of the event and the time of Esther's retrospective focalization of the event. In this image, however, the temporality, like the number of female figures, is tripled, recalling once again Jo's question: "Is there *three* of 'em, then?" In the time of the event, Lady Dedlock rushes forward, Esther sits, and Charley gathers flowers. In the time of the focalization, Esther remembers these events just as they happened and are described in her narrative. Hidden within this moment of focalization, however, and simultaneous with it are memories of two other "events" from Esther's past, of which the scene of "Lady Dedlock in the Wood" is just the manifest content, so to speak. Latent in this image of mother-daughter reunion is Esther's recollection of a very different scene from her own childhood, the burial of her doll in chapter 3 as she prepares to leave Windsor to go to school.

The visual clue that links the two scenes is the tree.[6] In chapter 3, Esther describes burying her doll as follows: "A day or two before, I had wrapped the dear old doll in her own shawl, and quietly laid her—I am half ashamed to tell it—in the garden earth, under the tree that shaded my old window" (36). The spot depicted in the illustration is not "in the park-woods of Chesney Wold" (576), as Esther calls them in her narrative, nor even "in the Wood," as the caption indicates, but beneath a single tree. Read as the memory of a different time, the figure of Charley innocently gathering flowers in the background becomes instead a memory of Esther herself, burying her doll.

The fact that Charley's face is hidden from view links her to Esther, whose face is also hidden, as it is in so many of the novel's illustrations. If Charley is the young Esther, however, her face may actually be present in the image—not on Esther's body, but on Lady Dedlock's, one face for the "*three* of 'em." Visual identification of a young female figure seen from the rear can perhaps never be absolutely certain, but in this case the fact that the depiction of Charley so closely resembles that of Esther in an illustration from the next monthly number in which she appears as narrator lends credibility to this claim. In "Sir Leicester Dedlock," from monthly number 14, Esther is also seen from behind, her face hidden, her hair up in a bun, her neck and shoulders in almost exactly the same posture as Charley's in the earlier image. That the figure of Charley in the background should be more faintly etched befits its status as a memory trace. The "real" event takes place in the foreground between the two more sharply delineated female figures; the memory hovers less distinctly in the background. As focalized retrospectively by Esther, the scene of maternal reunion triggers thoughts of a very different kind.

The missing face on Charley's body allows for other identifications as well. If we accept the possibility that Charley may be a memory trace of Esther burying her doll, then it is only a short step from this hypothesis to the suggestion that "Lady Dedlock in the Wood" contains another memory, or fantasy rather, that belongs to Esther. The scene of Charley picking flowers, I want to argue, disguises a scene from yet another time and place in Esther's story, the scene of the young Honoria Barbary burying the body of her infant daughter. Simply put, this is the novel's primal scene, Esther's unnarratable fantasy of origins, the "unthought known" that she can never quite put directly into words but that she seems compelled to repeat endlessly and that she manages here to visualize in condensed and displaced form. Divided structurally by the strong vertical tree trunk, the image juxtaposes two contradictory versions of maternal (and daughterly) response: a loving (and beloved) mother, eager to embrace her long-lost child, and a hateful (hated as well as hating) mother, eager to dispose of her unwanted infant's corpse.[7] Between the two images of her mother, Esther sits, remembers, dreams, fantasizes. In the foreground lies a broken limb torn from the parent tree, a reminder to the viewer and to Esther herself in retrospect of the violence latent in this otherwise peaceful scene.[8]

The idea that enables this entire line of speculation is the concept of focalization and of Esther as the retrospective focalizer of images like "Lady Dedlock in the Wood." The visual signs of retrospective focalization are roughly the equivalent, for many of the *Bleak House* illustrations, of the concept of voice, as it applies to Esther's retrospective narration. The uncanny repetitions and complex temporality that characterize Esther's narrative are thus also present in the novel's illustrations.

One final methodological point is worth making, whose relevance will become clear later. I said earlier that all the *Bleak House* illustrations can be understood as externally focalized—that is, as seen by a viewer who stands outside the depicted scene and who is not a character in the novel. This heteroperceptive viewpoint, I said, is roughly analogous though not identical to the perspective of the unnamed present-tense narrator in the verbal text. Thus, even those illustrations that I have argued are viewed by an unseen, character-based focalizer, such as "Lady Dedlock in the Wood," are also externally focalized. In other words, they have double focalization. It is also theoretically possible that, in addition to its external focalization, a given image may have more than one unseen, character-based focalizer. Under such conditions, triple focalization would be possible: an external heteroperceptive viewpoint and two (or more) unseen internal homoperceptive viewpoints.

In verbal narratives, the technical term used to indicate passages in which the narrator's speech and the speech of a character are indistinguishable is "free indirect discourse." In visual narratives, as Bal has pointed out, images exist in which external and character-based focalization are indistinguishable. *Bleak House* abounds in them. For such images, Bal has coined the term "free indirect perception."[9] In *Bleak House,* most of the instances of free indirect perception pertain to illustrations that correspond to passages narrated by Esther, and, as such, they are relatively unremarkable; that is, the illustrations are not significantly enriched or complicated by virtue of the fact that they can be understood as viewed simultaneously by an external focalizer and by the retrospective Esther. If, however, we were to find an example of an illustration that corresponds to a passage presented by the unnamed general narrator and that could also be read as focalized by the retrospective Esther, this would be highly significant, since it would entail the possibility that Esther knows, or sees, what the other narrator reports. It would mean, in other words, that the boundary separating the novel's two narrators and their narratives is to some extent permeable and that Esther is capable of crossing it. As we shall see, there is one illustration in *Bleak House* in which such a crossing of boundaries seems to occur.

3

PSYCHOANALYSIS

THE APPROACH THAT I HAVE ADOPTED THUS FAR TO READING Esther Woodcourt's narrative and to understanding some of the illustrations that I take to be focalized by her relies to a great extent implicitly on terms and concepts derived from psychoanalysis. It is time to make some of these concepts more explicit and to explore what I regard as the proto-psychoanalytic mythic structure that underlies the stories of Esther and her mother.

One important set of psychoanalytic ideas that informs my reading of Esther comes from trauma studies. The study of trauma and its effects on individual and collective memory has been a rich field of investigation since Freud and especially since his case study of the Wolf Man (written originally in 1914–15 and published in 1918) and his metapsychological paper *Beyond the Pleasure Principle* (1920). Freud's interest in trauma dates from his earliest papers on hysteria, jointly authored with Breuer. One direction of his thinking, much debated by later critics, concerns the so-called seduction theory and the question of whether patients' reports of early sexual abuse by parents or other adults were in fact real or merely fantasies. Freud's most important contributions to trauma theory, however, date from after World War I and grow largely out of his awareness of the problems experienced by soldiers suffering from war neuroses or shell shock. From these studies, and in papers such as "The Uncanny" (1919), he developed his important ideas about repetition compulsion and the return of the repressed. In footnotes added later to his Wolf Man case history, moreover, he returned to the question of whether traumatic memories (so-called primal scenes) were real or imagined. Unable finally to decide this question, he offered the concept of *Nachträglichkeit,* translated into English as "deferred action" and into French as *"après-coup,"* in order to deal with the hermeneutic undecidability posed by his analysis of the Wolf Man's famous dream. It does not matter, he concluded, whether the patient's observation of parental intercourse was the source of his neurosis or whether his later observation of animal copulation, projected retroactively upon the parents, served as the basis for a fantasy about them that subsequently appeared in the dream and functioned as an event. In either case, the result, the analysand's neurotic structure, is the same. In the latter case, however, normal temporal order would be reversed (the *Nachträglichkeit* effect), and a subsequent event could then be understood as the cause of a prior one. The concept of "deferred action" and of belatedness or "afterwardsness" more generally has greatly interested subsequent theorists in the fields of psychoanalysis, narratology, and epistemology.[1]

Important contributions to trauma studies have developed in the wake of other major historical catastrophes, notably the Holocaust, Hiroshima, and Vietnam, as well as in clinical treatment of patients suffering from the effects of childhood sexual abuse and other early emotional injuries. Post-traumatic stress disorder (PTSD) has become a widely recognized (and some would say overused) diagnostic category in the treatment of such individuals. The hypothesis of cross-generational transmission of trauma has also been proposed, especially in regard to the children of Holocaust survivors, but for other populations as well.[2]

Another influential model for understanding trauma, one that offers an interesting parallel to Freud's notion of *Nachträglichkeit,* has been developed by Robert Stolorow and his colleagues. Stolorow proposes a biphasic, relational model of trauma. According to this model, the original "traumatogenic" event is insufficient by itself to produce neurosis. "Pain is not pathology," Stolorow writes.[3] What produces pathology, he argues, is the lack of attuned responsiveness on the part of parents or other caregivers toward the child who suffers an unbearable affective injury. It is this later failure of response that "seals" the original injury and confers upon it a pathogenic power over the afflicted subject. In a sense, then, Stolorow's biphasic model, like *Nachträglichkeit*, attributes causal force to a subsequent experience that activates pathological power latent in the original wound. Unlike Freud, however, Stolorow does not question the reality of the original event.

Especially valuable for me in thinking about trauma in relation to *Bleak House* has been the work of Cathy Caruth. In *Unclaimed Experience: Trauma, Narrative, and History*, Caruth explores ways in which the texts of psychoanalysis, literature, and literary theory "both speak about and speak through the profound story of traumatic experience."[4] Drawing on Lacanian and post-Lacanian psychoanalysis and on deconstructive literary theory, especially the work of Derrida and Paul de Man, Caruth develops powerful readings of literary, filmic, and other texts that deal in one way or another with trauma. Her extensive footnotes provide a useful summary of prior work, sociological as well as psychoanalytic, in the field of trauma studies. Her concise accounts of trauma and its belated effects have direct relevance for understanding the predicament of Esther Summerson and the strange temporality of Esther Woodcourt's narrative. In language readily applicable to *Bleak House* as I have discussed it thus far, Caruth describes trauma as "an event that . . . is experienced too soon, too unexpectedly, to be fully known and is therefore not available to consciousness until it imposes itself again, repeatedly, in the nightmares and repetitive actions of the survivor" (4).

Particularly interesting for my purposes is Caruth's emphasis on voice and on the ways in which trauma speaks belatedly and from displaced sites of articulation. After citing an exemplary passage from Tasso's *Gerusalemme Liberata*, she writes, "What seems to me particularly striking in the example of Tasso is not just the unconscious act of the infliction of the injury and its inadvertent and unwished-for repetition, but the moving and sorrowful *voice* that cries out, a voice that is paradoxically released *through the wound*" (2; emphasis in the original). And again: "Trauma seems to be much more than a pathology, or the simple illness of a wounded psyche: it is always the story of a wound that cries out, that addresses us in the attempt to tell us of a reality or truth that is not otherwise available. This truth, in its delayed appearance and its belated address, cannot be linked only to what is known, but also to what remains unknown in our very actions and our language" (4). The uncanny repetitions, vocal displacement, belated address, and fugitive temporality that characterize Esther's retrospective narration are nicely summed up in this statement.

Both Freud's concept of *Nachträglichkeit* and Stolorow's biphasic model of trauma are relevant to Esther's situation. In Stolorow's terms, the traumatogenic event would be not so much Esther's birth itself as her sudden, violent separation from her mother, however this occurred. What seals the originary wound and gives it pathogenic force would be the godmother's lack of responsive attunement, her stern, unforgiving treatment of Esther throughout her infancy and early childhood. For Stolorow, it would be Miss Barbary's failure to respond, more than any action of Honoria's, that activates the trauma of Esther's birth and is chiefly responsible for her neurosis. Stolorow would thus presumably consider Esther's feelings toward her mother to be largely a transference from the godmother, though Lady Dedlock's subsequent lack of responsiveness, once her relationship to Esther becomes clear, would play a secondary role.

This Stolorovian account of Esther's neurosis can be supplemented by one that includes both a Freudian and a Lacanian and post-Lacanian emphasis on belatedness. The persistence in Esther's narrative of both verbal and visual fantasies of burial scenes argues for the relevance of Freud's *Nachträglichkeit* effect and particularly for the importance of the crucial scene in chapter 36 of Esther's reunion with her mother and her reaction to the letter that Lady Dedlock gives her. Of this letter Esther writes, once again putting Lady Dedlock's account into words of her own, "So strangely did I hold my place in this world, that, until within a short time back, I had never, to my own mother's knowledge, breathed—had been buried—had never been endowed with life—had never borne a name" (583). Esther's experience and recollection of her mother in this scene (and elsewhere) as cold and rejecting and as wishing Esther dead, reinforced by her earlier experience of her mother's sister, works retroactively to produce the powerful fantasy of infant burial, the novel's primal scene, which can in turn be read as Esther's point of origin and as the origin of her entire narrative. Whether this scene is "real" or merely imagined remains undecidable; the result, for Esther, is the same. For Esther Woodcourt, however, the experience and subsequent realization of her mother's "betrayal" of her in the reunion scene, reinforced by her later reading of the letter, color her narrative accounts of every interaction with Lady Dedlock and contribute to the complex temporality of these accounts, which are always overlaid with memories and fantasies of other "times and places."

In addition to ideas drawn from trauma studies, a second, perhaps less obvious, set of psychoanalytic concepts that undergirds my reading of Esther and Lady Dedlock derives from an important essay by psychoanalyst André Green entitled "The Dead Mother." The essay does not attempt to give a generalized account of the etiology and symptoms of traumatic neurosis. Instead, it describes a particular syndrome or complex, based on clinical observation, that originates, according to Green, in the infant's earliest affective relationship with the mother. The "dead mother" in Green's analysis is not literally dead. Rather, for a variety of reasons, such as bereavement or other significant loss, she is emotionally dead and thus not available to nurture and sustain her child. According to Green, the dead mother is a concept that refers to

> an imago which has been constituted in the child's mind, following maternal depression, brutally transforming a living object, which was a source of vitality for the child, into a distant figure, toneless, practically inanimate, deeply impregnating the cathexes of certain patients whom we have in analysis, and weighing on the destiny of their object-libidinal and narcissistic future. Thus, the dead mother, contrary to what one might think, is a mother who remains alive but who is, so to speak, psychically dead in the eyes of the young child in her care.[5]

For Green, the problem at the core of the dead mother complex is depression, but depression, he says, comes in two colors: black and white. The black depression belongs to the mother, whose incomplete mourning over her loss results in an extended form of melancholy. For the infant, and for the child and adult that it becomes, depression takes the form of blankness. (Writing in French, Green puns on the word *blanc*, which means "blank" as well as "white.") The category of "blankness" for Green manifests itself in a variety of ways: "negative hallucination, blank psychosis, blank mourning, all connected to what one might call the problem of emptiness, or of the negative" (146). Blankness also leaves traces in the unconscious in the form of what he calls "psychical holes" (146). "*The essential character of this depression,*" he writes, "*is that it takes place in the presence of the object, which is itself depressed.* The mother, for one reason or another, is depressed" (149; emphasis in the original).

Green suggests several possible reasons for the mother's depression: "the loss of a person dear to her . . . , a deception which inflicts a narcissistic wound: a change of fortune in the nuclear family or family of origin," and so on. "In any event the mother's sorrow and lessening of interest in her infant are in the foreground. . . . It should be noted," he continues, "that the most serious instance [of maternal depression] is the death of a child at an early age" (149). In response to the mother's depression or "death," the infant first tries in vain to repair the mother and bring her back to life again. Failing in this attempt, the infant adopts a series of defensive strategies for dealing with what it experiences as a catastrophic loss of love. One defense is a "unique movement with two aspects: *the decathexis of the maternal object and the unconscious identification with the dead mother.* The decathexis," Green continues, "which is principally affective, but also representative, constitutes a psychical murder of the object, accomplished without hatred" (151–52; emphasis in the original).

The second aspect of this defense, according to Green, is a "mirror-identification" with the mother. "This reactive symmetry is the only means by which to establish a reunion with the mother—perhaps by way of sympathy. In fact there is no real reparation, but a mimicry, with the aim of continuing to possess the object (who[m] one can no longer have) by becoming, not like it but, the object itself" (151). In addition to identification with the dead mother, a second defensive reaction to the loss of maternal love, Green says, is "*the loss of meaning*" (151; emphasis in the original). The infant blames itself for the mother's "death" and comes to "imagine this fault to be linked to [its] manner of being rather than with some forbidden wish; in fact, it becomes forbidden for [it] to be" (151–52). This position, Green concludes, "could induce the child to let [itself] die" (152).[6]

As is no doubt already apparent, Green's formulation of the dead mother complex has remarkable affinities to the situation we find in *Bleak House*. The uncaring, unresponsive, "dead mother" imago is spread across several maternal figures in the book, including Mrs. Rachael, Mrs. Jellyby, and Mrs. Pardiggle, as well as of course Miss Barbary. For Esther, however, as well as for the other narrator, the dead mother imago settles primarily on Lady Dedlock. From the outset, we learn that Lady Dedlock is, in her own words, "bored to death" (21) and that, like Alexander, who "wept when he had no more worlds to conquer, . . . my Lady Dedlock, having conquered *her* world, fell, not into the melting but rather into the freezing mood" (22). It is worth noting in passing that the other narrator's repeated and ironic use of the first-person possessive pronoun "my" when referring to Lady Dedlock is an instance of free indirect discourse. In addition to the narrator's own ironic usage, the phrase "my lady" is the mocking quotation of an expression, at once deferential and at times overly familiar, adopted by servants and shopkeepers, indeed by everyone who knows her and seeks favor in her eyes or who wishes to slyly denigrate her arrogant demeanor. In its first-person address, moreover, it is also a faint reminder of Esther's own first-person narrative and of her ardent but impossible wish also to claim Lady Dedlock as "my lady."

Frozen, bored to death, hiding behind a mask of "careless" aristocratic hauteur, Lady Dedlock is emotionally dead from the first scene in which she appears. On closer examination, it is easy to recognize her condition as one of protracted melancholy. Although married to one of the most exalted members of the aristocracy, she suffers from depression, depression over the double loss of her lover (Captain Hawdon) and of the child she conceived by him. Although sealed off from her present existence and hidden from the view of others, the secret of her past and of this double bereavement remains acutely alive within her, ready to be activated by the smallest reminder. When she sees the evidence of Hawdon's handwriting in chapter 2, she is suddenly shaken. Tulkinghorn, always quick to notice, remarks that Lady Dedlock is ill. "'Faint,' my Lady murmurs, with white lips, 'only that; but it is like the faintness of death'" (27).

Guarded, emotionally distant except in her relationship with the daughter surrogate Rosa, Lady Dedlock shades her face from view. The shadow that falls upon her, however, and that we see most clearly in the illustration of "The Young Man of the name of Guppy" (fig. 8), is the same shadow of which Freud speaks in his famous characterization of melancholy: "The shadow of the object fell upon the ego."[7] Once Lady Dedlock reappears in Esther's life and announces herself as Esther's mother, her frozen, haughty demeanor recapitulates Esther's early experience of the godmother and becomes the focus of her fantasies as well as of her actual experience and retrospective accounts of Lady Dedlock.

FIG. 8. "The Young Man of the name of Guppy."

If Lady Dedlock is the "dead mother" of Green's formulation, Esther is the daughter who tries in vain to revive the frozen mother, to warm her heart and restore her to vitality so that she can in turn nurture and sustain the daughter who has pined so long for her affection. Failing in this effort, Esther takes the blame upon herself and vows, as she tells her doll in chapter 3, "to repair the fault I had been born with (of which I confusedly felt guilty and yet innocent), and . . . [to] strive as I grew up to be industrious, contented and kind-hearted, and to do some good to some one, and win some love to myself if I could" (31). Thus is born Esther's second self, the inauthentic identity I have called "Good Esther." Hidden beneath this dutiful persona are two other Esthers. One is the daughter who suffers from what Green calls a "blank depression," who experiences a loss of meaning in her life and "psychical holes" in her unconscious, and for whom it is forbidden to be. The other Esther is a darker, ghostly self that emerges often in the night and who, in her role as narrator, is endowed with a powerful, resonant voice that often breaks out whenever thoughts of her mother are nearby.

Blankness, however, is the condition that most commonly afflicts Esther, especially when she looks in the mirror or in the mirror of another face. In the opening paragraph of her first chapter, Esther describes her doll, who "used to sit propped up in a great arm-chair, with her beautiful complexion and rosy lips, staring at me—or not so much at me, I think, as at nothing,—while I busily stitched away, and told her every one of my secrets" (27–28). The doll stares at "nothing" because the doll is inanimate; its eyes are incapable of focus. In this respect it is a version of the dead mother, also inanimate, also incapable of seeing or responding to the needful child. The doll is beautiful, like the mother, like Esther herself, and like Ada, that other doll-like beauty whose "darling" face Esther cherishes so fondly; but when Esther remembers the doll looking at her, she recalls it staring at "nothing"—that is, not at Esther's beautiful face, but at the "psychical hole" where Esther's self should be.

Esther always has trouble with mirrors. They are an invitation to vanity, which she modestly avoids, but they are also dangerous, because they remind her that she is beautiful and thus sexually attractive and not just a little old lady whom no one need regard. Mirrors are also dangerous because they potentially threaten to confirm her deepest fear—that she does not exist, that in the place of her face there is "nothing." When she first visits Kenge and Carboy's prior to going before the Lord Chancellor, for example, Guppy, who has already spotted her as a beautiful young thing, calls her attention to a little looking-glass, "In case you should wish to look at yourself, miss, after the journey." Esther picks up a newspaper and begins to read, but, after a brief moment of dissociation, in which "I . . . found myself reading the same words repeatedly" (notice Esther's use of the reflexive verb here, often a sign of psychic splitting), "I put the paper down, took a peep at my bonnet in the glass to see if it was neat, and looked at the room" (43). Esther looks at her bonnet, but not at her face, worried perhaps that she may find nothing there.

Among the novel's many other scenes of mirroring, the most memorable is the one from the crucial chapter 36 in which Esther first looks at her face in the glass following the illness that leaves her scarred beyond recognition. After Charley brings her the mirror, she first veils herself with her long, thick hair, then slowly lifts a muslin curtain drawn across the glass, before parting her hair and looking at her face. "I drew [the curtain] back; and stood for a moment looking through such a veil of my own hair, that I could see nothing else" (572). She sees her hair, but she also sees "nothing else"—a blankness that is unsettling because strange, but that she somehow finds reassuring since it means that she may no longer pose the danger of exposure to her mother.[8] Putting her hair aside, she contemplates her face, but, as in the early scene at Kenge and Carboy's, she gives us no details, only the sense of strangeness and then gradual familiarity that takes its place as she grows accustomed to the alteration in her looks and comes to "know" it (I suspect that the verb she means is "like") "better than I had done at first." "It was not like what I had expected," she writes, "but I had expected nothing definite, and I dare say anything definite would have surprised me" (572). The willed operation of self-disfigurement has been successful, and Esther's face has been replaced by "nothing definite."

By destroying her face, Esther in effect destroys her self, or rather, restores it to an already familiar and desired blankness—the blank look of the doll, but without its beauty. In so doing, she not only complies with what she imagines to be her mother's unspoken wish; she also identifies with her mother—adopting, like Lady Dedlock, a mask of impassivity, a mask of death, in order to protect the secret of their common past. While there may be something reassuring for her about this "reactive symmetry," as Green calls it, identification with the dead mother is also a deeply terrifying experience, as the dreams Esther reports having had during her illness make abundantly clear. These dreams—of "labouring" up endless stairs like a worm, only to be turned back and forced to repeat the task again, and of being a bead on a flaming necklace and praying only to be taken off from the rest (555–56)—lend themselves to multiple interpretations: the labor of birth, the labor of repeatedly performing the abject role of "Good Esther," but also suicide and self-annihilation. However we interpret them, they are evidence of what Green calls the "loss of meaning" whose manifestations include "negative hallucination, blank psychosis, blank mourning, all connected to what one might call the problem of emptiness, or of the negative."

Esther's reunion with her mother in chapter 36 briefly offers the hope of a possible escape from the agony of the "negative," but, as we have seen, Lady Dedlock's ambivalent response in this scene and her equally ambiguous letter leave Esther uncertain at best about what her future holds. Instead, she turns, as she has done before, to another source of comfort, her "darling" Ada. The scene of her reunion with Ada functions as an opportunity both for Esther Summerson to replay the unsatisfactory reunion scene with her mother experienced only the previous day, and for Esther Woodcourt to reexperience and rework both scenes in retrospect. I have already discussed the way in which Esther's anticipation of seeing Ada for the first time after her illness, running down the road toward her and then dashing back to hide in her room, repeats larger rhythms and patterns of movement in her narrative as a whole. What remains to be analyzed is the Ada reunion scene itself, especially the strange way in which it ends—with Ada and Esther embracing each other passionately on the floor.

The reunion scene with Ada is multivalent and lends itself to a range of interpretations. For my purposes, the main significance of the scene lies in its juxtaposition to the preceding scene of failed reunion between Esther and her mother. As Dever convincingly shows, the scene between Esther and Lady Dedlock is a farewell scene rather than one of reconnection. Lady Dedlock tells Esther to consider her "evermore . . . as dead" (580; note that these are Esther's words, not direct speech by Lady Dedlock). The supposed reunion scene with the mother and the letter that follows it are in fact a betrayal of the mother-daughter bond, and it is this sense of betrayal that governs Esther Woodcourt's retrospective account of the event.

Having failed to achieve a satisfactory reunion with her mother, Esther understandably looks to her dearest friend for support and consolation, but here too she has doubts and fears. If complying with her imagined idea of the mother's wish that she destroy the facial resemblance between them has not succeeded in winning the mother's love, how will her friend Ada respond to the scarred face that she now presents? Her uncertainty is understandable and becomes palpable in her erratic movements back and forth along the lane where Ada is expected. When she does arrive, however, Ada's reaction to seeing her friend again appears to be everything, and more, that Esther could have hoped for. Here is Esther's account of the scene:

> She ran in, and was running out again when she saw me. Ah, my angel girl! the old dear look, all love, all fondness, all affection. Nothing else in it—no, nothing, nothing!
>
> O how happy I was, down upon the floor, with my sweet beautiful girl down upon the floor too, holding my scarred face to her lovely cheek, bathing it with tears and kisses, rocking me to and fro like a child, calling me by every tender name that she could think of, and pressing me to her faithful heart. (588)

Three points about this scene are worth noting. First is the way in which it allows Esther to replay in a different key the failed reunion scene with her mother. Ada here takes the part of Lady Dedlock, providing Esther with the unconditional acceptance and love that her mother has been unable or unwilling to give. She holds Esther in her arms, bathes her scarred face with kisses and tears, and rocks her to and fro "like a child." (Dickens originally wrote "infant" here, but replaced it with the word "child."[9]) Secondly, the scene allows Esther as narrator both to reexperience the comforting reaction of her friend and at the same time to express indirectly her anger at Lady Dedlock for her betrayal in the scene that Esther has narrated only a few pages before. The key word here is "faithful." We may recall that among the first words that Esther reports herself as having said, long ago at the beginning of chapter 3, were "O you dear faithful Dolly, I knew you would be expecting me!" (28). In her childish play, Esther uses Dolly as a mother substitute, a mother who expects her child home after school, who wants to listen to "every one of my secrets," a mother who is "faithful." The mother who finally reveals herself to Esther in chapter 36, and whom Esther Woodcourt has more critically observed during the course of her entire narrative, has certainly not been "expecting" Esther to reappear in her life, however, and is anything but "faithful." When Esther writes that Ada presses her "to her faithful heart," she is commenting obliquely on her mother's lack of faithfulness, both in the earlier reunion scene and throughout Esther's entire life.

Faithfulness and its opposite, betrayal, are a major theme that runs through the whole of *Bleak House,* from the failure of Chancery to administer justice under the law and in particular to exercise responsibility toward the orphans in its charge, to Skimpole's and Turveydrop's irresponsible paternity, to the various bad mothers sprinkled throughout the book, to society's betrayal of Jo and the likes of Jo who hover, neglected, on its margins. Pervasive as its indictment of both individual and social betrayal may be, the novel is not entirely pessimistic on this score. It does contain several notable counterexamples of faithfulness that, while they do not offset the larger patterns of betrayal in the book, nevertheless offer some limited reason for hope. In this connection, we may recall Mrs. Rouncewell's long history of faithful service to the Dedlock family as well as her loyalty to and willingness to forgive her prodigal son George; the Bagnets, both in their strong family bonds (the only intact, loving family in the book) and in their willingness to stand surety for George's loan; George's soldierly loyalty to Sir Leicester at the end of the book; Sir Leicester's surprising and touching formal declaration of fidelity to Lady Dedlock, even after Bucket has provided him with the information about her past; Mr. Snagsby's willingness to continue shedding half-crowns to Jo, despite his wife's suspicious disapproval; Guster's simple kindness to Jo; and, perhaps most touching of all, Nemo's charity to Jo and Jo's reciprocal gift to him of the only things he has to offer: his labor—sweeping the graveyard step—and his words—"He was wery good to me, he wos."

These acts of common decency and basic human solidarity, performed mostly by and between members of the lower classes (with the wonderful exception of Sir Leicester), stand in striking contrast to the negligence and disloyalty of most members of the middle and upper classes, who practice only "telescopic philanthropy" if any philanthropy at all. They contrast particularly with the actions of Chadband, who masquerades as a spokesman for Christian brotherhood, but serves only himself, as well as those of Tulkinghorn, who masquerades as the aristocracy's faithful retainer, but actually holds them in sinister contempt. They contrast also with the actions of Lady Dedlock, whose "betrayal" of Esther, not so much at the time of giving birth as in her refusal to recognize, accept, and embrace her daughter once her existence has been revealed, stands as the chief individual "crime" in this novel of pervasive social criminality.

A third and final point to note about the scene of Esther's reunion with Ada is a troubling undercurrent that runs counter to the reassurance offered by Ada's comforting response. Ada starts to run out of the room, but sees Esther and turns back. Recalling this precious moment in her narrative, Esther writes, in exclamatory verbless phrases that have no temporality, "Ah, my angel girl! the old dear look, all love, all fondness, all affection. Nothing else in it—no, nothing, nothing!" What troubles a reader attentive to Esther's voice in this passage is the persistence, alongside the indications of love, fondness, and affection, of the repeated negative term "nothing." What Esther sees in the mirror of Ada's face is "the old dear look"—a look that is "old" and whose location is impossible to fix, since it is a look exchanged and shared between them, a mirror image. At the same time that the look offers reassurance and love, it also summons up, probably unconsciously for Esther as narrator, memories of blankness, of her doll, of the dead mother. Even in the time of writing, Esther remains haunted by the fear that her face and her personhood have "nothing else in it—no, nothing, nothing!"

At the beginning of this chapter I alluded to the presence of "a proto-psychoanalytic mythic structure" in *Bleak House,* and it is to this topic that I now want to turn as a way of concluding my discussion of "psychoanalysis" in the novel. I use the terms "myth" and "mythic structure" advisedly, for I want to argue that the novel explicitly invokes a well-known classical myth and uses it, in two slightly different versions, in order to explore intersubjective and intrapsychic phenomena that have a remarkable similarity to the process of psychoanalysis. The myth I have in mind is the story of Proserpine or, in Greek, Persephone.

The closest the novel comes to a direct allusion to this myth occurs near the beginning of chapter 22 in a remarkable passage describing the solitary pleasure that Mr. Tulkinghorn, at home in Lincoln's Inn Fields, takes in the consumption of port. I quote the paragraph in its entirety.

> In his lowering magazine of dust, the universal article into which his paper and himself, and all his clients, and all things of earth, animate and inanimate, are resolving, Mr. Tulkinghorn sits at one of the open windows, enjoying a bottle of old port. Though a hard-grained man, close, dry, and silent, he can enjoy old wine with the best. He has a priceless binn of port in some artful cellar under the Fields, which is one of his many secrets. When he dines alone in chambers, as he has dined today, and has his bit of fish and his steak or chicken brought in from the coffee-house, he descends with a candle to the echoing regions below the deserted mansion, and, heralded by a remote reverberation of thundering doors, comes gravely back, encircled by an earthy atmosphere, and carrying a bottle from which he pours a radiant nectar, two score and ten years old, that blushes in the glass to find itself so famous, and fills the whole room with the fragrance of southern grapes. (352)

As this passage clearly suggests, Tulkinghorn is a figure of death or, to be more specific, of Hades or Pluto. The kingdom over which he rules is the underworld, to which he descends periodically in search of the blushing bottle of port, and from which he comes "gravely" back, bearing the sweet wine that he then sips with the pleasure of a connoisseur. The blushing bottle is Proserpine, his queen, whose cyclical ascent and return down beneath "the Fields" repeats the seasonal cycle of fertility and cold. The presence of the Roman figure of Allegory painted on the ceiling of his chambers and pointing down at him is one clue to the possibility that Tulkinghorn himself may be a figure of allegorical or mythic dimensions.

The language of the passage is extraordinarily sensuous, Keatsian even, and begs to be read aloud so that the reader can savor, vicariously with Tulkinghorn, the sweetness he imbibes. We do not usually think of Tulkinghorn as a sensualist, but here, observing him alone, the narrator captures something essential in his nature. Readers have often wondered about Tulkinghorn's motives in tracking down Lady Dedlock's secret and threatening her with exposure. What does he hope to gain from his blackmail scheme? Not money or even power, I suspect, unless perhaps over her. The passage from chapter 22 helps to explain what he is after. He does not really want to expose Lady Dedlock's secret, nor even to use his power over her to manipulate Sir Leicester. What he wants is to possess Lady Dedlock, to add her to his store of sweet, blushing secrets and bring her up periodically to sip and torture with vampirish delight. Outwardly a misogynist who shuns and distrusts women, inhabiting a world only of men, Tulkinghorn is also a sadist who takes erotic pleasure in punishing women and keeping them under his control. The game of emotional chess he plays with Lady Dedlock is designed not to end in checkmate but by capturing the queen and holding her in thrall. (In another "allegorical" pattern, Tulkinghorn is the rook, Lady Dedlock the restless queen, always on the move, and Sir Leicester the powerless king, immobilized by gout and later by his stroke.) She remains free to move about the country but always under his sway, allowing the game to continue indefinitely.

What does any of this have to do with psychoanalysis? Very little, or perhaps only this. Tulkinghorn is a lawyer, hired by Sir Leicester to provide professional service to the Dedlock family. In the course of his duties, he inevitably acquires knowledge of the family's secrets. Like the psychoanalyst, who also acquires his client's secrets, the lawyer is presumably bound by a contract of confidentiality and, again like the analyst, uses his professional skills only to further his client's interests and not for any personal gain beyond the monetary reward specified in the terms of their contract. In coveting his employer's wife, Tulkinghorn exceeds the terms of his contract and violates his employer's trust, recalling the Oedipal dynamics of another trusted employee, Carker, in

Dombey and Son. The key difference between Tulkinghorn and the psychoanalyst is that Tulkinghorn uses his professional knowledge to torture Lady Dedlock, not to help her.

The mythic structure established in the passage from chapter 22, with Tulkinghorn as Hades or Pluto and Lady Dedlock as Proserpine, is repeated with a difference in the relationship between Bucket and Esther. Like Tulkinghorn, Bucket is a professional in the employ of Sir Leicester, though previously he had worked for Tulkinghorn. Unlike Tulkinghorn, Bucket maintains a properly professional demeanor and does not allow personal motives, other than well-deserved professional pride and the expectation of his fee, to interfere with the execution of his detective duties. In his professional capacity, he performs various tasks, among them solving the murder of Tulkinghorn, arresting the murderess, discovering the whereabouts of Lady Dedlock, and recovering the letters she wrote to Captain Hawdon, thereby neutralizing the threat of blackmail but incidentally exposing her secret and thus precipitating Sir Leicester's stroke. His most important part in the mythic structure of the book, however, is the role of Orpheus that he plays in relation to Esther, who here functions as Eurydice.

The Orpheus-Eurydice story, as classical scholars have long recognized, is a variant of the Proserpine myth. A beautiful young woman dies, bitten by a snake, and descends into the underworld. Her lover, determined to recover her, travels down into the world of death and tries to bring her back. Unlike the lord of the underworld, who wishes to retain his queen forever in thrall and allows her only periodic escapes to the upper world, Orpheus seeks to liberate Eurydice and bring her back permanently to a world where she can flourish and experience love. Unfortunately, he is ultimately unsuccessful in this task.

The role of Orpheus, as I have briefly sketched it here, resembles that of the psychoanalyst who accompanies his patient down into the world of the unconscious, wanders with her there, searching for clues that will enable her to escape from the prison of her neurosis, locates, if he is lucky, the path that will enable her to find her way back up to the surface, allows his reassuring presence to help her on her way, and then finally releases her to take the final steps on her own, since no one other than the patient can work through and master the conflicts that have imprisoned her, so to speak, in the realm of the living dead. In the somewhat anachronistic analogy I am proposing, Bucket performs the role of psychoanalyst for Esther, or rather of Orpheus, going down into the depths of her soul and accompanying her, following as well as leading, on her difficult path toward recovery. The extent to which he and they succeed remains to be seen.

If I am correct in suggesting that in *Bleak House* Dickens was revisiting the story of Orpheus and Eurydice, what is most extraordinary in the novel's handling of the myth is that Dickens allows the story to be told by and from the perspective of Eurydice. Or, to press my psychoanalytic analogy still further, *Bleak House* is the story of a psychoanalysis, complete with episodes of extreme dissociation and even psychosis, narrated by the patient.

When Bucket first comes for Esther to seek her help in searching for Lady Dedlock, it is in the middle of the night. Awakened from sleep, Esther goes with him, and the rest of their journey unfolds as if in a dream. The object of their search, as both of them recognize, is Esther's mother, but it is equally Esther herself. The rescue project that Bucket undertakes has Lady Dedlock as its initial goal, but it soon becomes a project of rescuing Esther as well. Likewise for Esther, though she does not recognize it consciously at the time, finding her mother is a way to find herself. She is in pursuit not only of the lost bond of affection with her mother, but also of the face that she dimly recalls from infancy, "the first thing in the world I had ever seen." The face is also her own, sometimes beautiful like Ada's, but more often blank like Dolly's, staring "not so much at me, I think, as at nothing." In order to recover her beauty and vitality, in order to return from the land of the living dead, Esther must confront the blankness of the negative, must look her "dead mother" fully in the face. Before there can be any hope of rescue, Eurydice must somehow acknowledge and come to terms with the fact that she is dead.

The earliest parts of Esther's journey are the most regressed and the most frightening.[10] Bucket first takes her down by the river, thinking that her mother may have thrown herself into the Thames. Literally, he is mistaken, of course, but Esther's hallucinatory description of these scenes (always in retrospect, but focalized through her younger self) suggests that what Bucket finds there may in fact be part of what they are looking for. After descending through a labyrinth of streets, crossing and recrossing the river, they arrive at "a little slimy turning, which the wind from the river, rushing up it, did not purify" (868). Recalling the scene in retrospect, Esther re-creates syntactically, by the use of a reflexive verb and a strategically placed prepositional phrase, her experience of dissociation, of being at the same time present and not present at an encounter with some secret, abjected part of the self: "*I had no need to remind myself that I was not there,* by the indulgence of any feeling of mine, to increase the difficulties of the search" (869; emphasis mine). As if in "the horror of a dream" that she still "never can forget," Esther recalls that "a man yet dark and muddy, in long swollen sodden boots and with a hat like them, . . . whispered with Mr. Bucket, who went away with him down some slippery steps—as if to look at something secret that he had to show. They came back, wiping their hands upon their coats, after turning over something wet; but thank God it was not what I feared!" (869). The slimy "something" is not her mother, but it may be a part of herself.

The process of descent into the depths of the unconscious continues under Bucket's watchful eye. He gazes "into the profound black pit of water, with a face that made my heart die within me." As she writes, Esther's prose richens and darkens; it becomes powerful in the way that it does whenever she gains access to unconscious modes of thought.

> The river had a fearful look, so overcast and secret, creeping away so fast between the low flat lines of shore: so heavy with indistinct and awful shapes, both of substance and shadow: so deathlike and mysterious. I have seen it many times since then, by sunlight and by moonlight, but never free from the impressions of that journey. In my memory, the lights upon the bridge are always burning dim; the cutting wind is eddying round the homeless woman whom we pass; the monotonous wheels are whirling on; and the light of the carriage lamps reflected back, looks palely in upon me—a face, rising out of the dreaded water. (870)

In this extraordinary passage, full of primary process thinking and marked by a shift into the present tense of recollection, Esther/Eurydice conveys what it felt like at the time, and still feels like in her haunted memory now, to wander in the realm of the dead. The face that she sees "rising out of the dreaded water" is her mother's, but of course also her own.

Meanwhile, Bucket remains alert and watchful, at times almost cheerful, and it is worth paying close attention to the way in which he conducts his investigation, both what he says (always as reported by Esther) and what she remembers of his mannerisms and gestures. We have already observed Bucket on several occasions earlier in the book, in chapters told by the other narrator, and his interactions with Esther are generally consistent with his behavior in those contexts. He maintains an easy, garrulous manner with people of every class and background while at the same time keeping an eye out for any detail that might prove helpful in his search. Several small habits of speech and gesture deserve notice. One is his trick of calling people by their name. Almost every time he speaks to Esther, he calls her "Miss Summerson" or "my dear" and once, after he has realized that Lady Dedlock and Jenny have switched clothes, even "my darling" (885). (We find the same device in chapter 56, where Bucket repeatedly addresses the paralyzed Sir Leicester by his full name and title, "Sir Leicester Dedlock, Baronet.") Another little verbal tic is his habit of beginning sentences with the adverb "Now." "Why, now, I'll tell you, Miss Summerson," he begins in typical fashion, as he launches into one of his stories. Yet another mannerism is his habit of asking Esther how she is doing—"Are you well wrapped up, Miss Summerson?"—and offering polite little reassuring comments that often sound trite: "'It may be a long job,' he observed; 'but so that it ends well, never mind, miss'" (868). Somewhat more unusual is his kindly but slightly intrusive way of telling Esther what she feels. When he hands her a cup of tea at one of their stops, for example, he says, "Drink it, Miss Summerson, it'll do you good. You're beginning to get more yourself now, ain't you?" (872). More curious yet is his habit of telling Esther who he is: "You know me, my dear; now, don't you?" and again, "Inspector Bucket. Now you know me, don't you?" (885).

Colloquial, jocular, slightly comic in their redundancy, these mannerisms of speech serve another, more serious purpose. They are Bucket's way of maintaining contact with Esther during her arduous descent; they keep him attuned to her in the present time, the "now," of their journey. Largely phatic in their address, they have little content other than to tell Esther who he is and who she is and that she can rely on him to stay with her no matter how long or difficult their trip may be. More important than the content of what he says—those homely moral bromides—are the sustained contact and empathic attunement his verbal mannerisms provide.

Bucket's speech mannerisms are accompanied by a repertoire of nonverbal gestures. He uses his finger as a directional pointer, the finger that the other narrator has already endowed with semi-magical qualities. He never leaves Esther alone, but keeps coming back to her in the carriage to report on what he has seen or learned. Most important of all, in terms of the book's major pattern of visual recognition, he lends Esther his face. She refers regularly to his face, and it is his face more than his words that she reads for evidence of how the investigation is proceeding. In his regular rhythm of going away and coming back, going away and coming back, Bucket stages his own game of "peek-a-boo" for Esther's benefit. This is a version of the famous *Fort/Da* game of absence and presence that Freud describes in *Beyond the Pleasure Principle*, in which the infant learns to master the trauma of maternal separation and develop the capacity to be alone without anxiety. In his constant attention, his attunement to her feeling states, and his willingness to offer her the reassurance of his face, Bucket functions as Esther's analyst, capitalizing on her maternal transference to him in order to do for her what no mother ever did and thus help bring her back toward life.

This versatile repertoire of verbal and nonverbal response is part of Bucket's "technique," both as detective and, in the analogy I have been pursuing, as psychoanalyst. We could even say, if the term were not too grand, that it is his song. Bucket is a homely Orpheus. (Recall that when he takes Hortense away in a cloud of smoke at the end of the exposure scene in chapter 54, the other narrator calls him a "homely Jupiter" [837].) "Now I am not a poetical man myself," he tells Esther in one of his digressions during their ride, "except in a vocal way when it goes round a company" (875). In chapter 49, before placing George under arrest, Bucket joins the musical Bagnets in a chorus of "Brit Ish Gra-a-anadeers!" and, in one of the few revelations he makes about his private life (assuming he is to be believed here more than in the other stories he invents about himself), he "confess[es] how that he did once chaunt a little, for the expression of the feelings of his own bosom." He goes on to tell Mrs. Bagnet that he considers his rendition of the ballad "Believe Me If All Those Endearing Young Charms" to have been "his most powerful ally in moving the heart of Mrs. Bucket when a maiden, and inducing her to approach the altar" (763). Along with Little Swills, Bucket is the novel's other accomplished vocalist, and in this respect he is a plausible, if somewhat unlikely and ludic, candidate for the role of Orpheus.

Chapter 59, the one that always makes me weep, brings Esther's journey to a close. Bucket has a smaller role to play here; he has already done his work. When he realizes that Lady Dedlock and Jenny have switched places, he turns and follows what he calls "the other" (884). This decision means that instead of pursuing the substitute deeper "down" into the country, away from the city, he and Esther will go "up" toward London, as he insistently tells the stable hand: "Up, I tell you! Up! An't it English? Up!" (884). Having started down by the river's slimy edge, they now head back out of the depths of the unconscious toward the conscious realization that Esther must make when she reaches the burial ground. Bucket's most interesting intervention during this part of the journey is to reassure Esther that she is "a pattern, you know, that's what you are," adding, "My dear, . . . when a young lady is as mild as she's game, and as game as she's mild, that's all I ask, and more than I expect. She then becomes a Queen, and that's about what you are yourself" (902). Bucket's homely compliment summons Esther to her true identity as biblical queen, the young and beautiful self that awaits her at the end of her journey toward health.

The rest of the journey Esther must make chiefly on her own. She becomes more active, helping Bucket to retrieve her mother's final letter from the Snagsbys' orphan servant and commiserating with her, "laying my face against her forehead" (911) as poor Guster recovers from a seizure. Mirroring the orphan servant girl, Esther too seems headed toward recovery. As they get closer to the graveyard where Esther's father is buried and where Lady Dedlock will end her life, Esther must go on foot. They are joined by the physician Allan Woodcourt, but even he, Esther's friend and future husband, is not permitted to go the last few steps with her to where the body lies. Esther, meanwhile, has not allowed herself to think of what lies ahead of her. She remains fixated on the phrase "the mother of the dead child," believing that ahead of them is Jenny, who will tell them where to find her mother. Unconsciously, of course, Esther knows whose body it is, and Esther Woodcourt has known all along that the journey can end nowhere else.

As she approaches the body, struggling against the knowledge she cannot escape, Esther's internal world begins to strain and collapse. Remembering and reexperiencing this awful moment, Esther undergoes a seizure of her own. She writes "that the stained house fronts put on human shapes and looked at me; that great water-gates seemed to be opening and closing in my head, or in the air; and that the unreal things were more substantial than the real" (913). The phrase "the mother of the dead child" is the key to the mystery. Esther is the dead child, and when she lifts the head, parts the hair, and turns the face, what she sees is the dead mother and her own dead self.

4
ENDINGS

THE ONLY WAY THAT LADY DEDLOCK CAN ESCAPE FROM THE lord of the underworld who controls her secret is to renounce secrecy altogether. To do so is to cast off her identity as grand lady, the frozen mask of boredom that has imprisoned her in a state of deadlock and kept her from living or loving. Paradoxically, the first real act of love that she performs is a repetition of her greatest crime, the rejection of a daughter. When she turns Rosa away from Chesney Wold, however, it is not out of indifference or shame, but to save the girl and allow her to have a future of happiness with the man she loves. Renouncing secrecy also means leaving Sir Leicester, but in stripping herself of his jewels and relinquishing her watch, and in exchanging clothes with "the mother of the dead child," Lady Dedlock is embracing the painful but more authentic identity that she has tried so long to escape. Changing clothes with Jenny also means becoming homeless; it means accepting her place as, in Guster's words, "a common-looking person, all wet and muddy" (911).

One measure of the extent to which Lady Dedlock has renounced her former identity and embraced "common" humanity is her interaction with the Snagsbys' serving girl. Because she does not know how to find the burial ground on her own, she must ask for directions, as she did once before of Jo. Guster tells her how to find the graveyard and agrees to take the letter that she leaves for Esther. "And so I took it from her," Guster says, "and she said she had nothing to give me, and I said I was poor myself and consequently wanted nothing. And so she said God bless you! And went" (912). In her earlier visit to the graveyard, Lady Dedlock had paid her guide, but never thanked him—vanishing without speaking and leaving behind only the useless gold sovereign that Jo is never able to spend and that brings him more trouble than good. Here, with Guster, she abandons the cash nexus system and enters instead into the economy of the gift, the economy of the poor, who have nothing and want nothing. The blessing that she leaves for Guster repeats and corrects in a finer tone her earlier arrogant and thankless treatment of Jo.

Renouncing the regime of secrecy also means that Lady Dedlock must die—of cold, wet, and fatigue, but also, as she tells Esther in her final letter, "of terror and my conscience" (910). She is terrified, no longer of Tulkinghorn, of whose murder she learns from Mrs. Rouncewell, but of the social disgrace and shame that await her if she attempts to continue a life as Lady Dedlock. She is conscience-stricken over the effects that she fears scandal will have on Sir Leicester, but also, and more profoundly, at the knowledge of what she has done to Esther. Nevertheless, in death, or rather in dying, she has become more alive than at any other time when we observe her, and her final words, "Farewell. Forgive," may be the most authentic she has ever produced.

For Esther, the end of chapter 59 is not an ending; it is a beginning, the beginning of a new life. But what are we to make of the life that she reports living? And how successful has her homely Orpheus been in bringing her back from the underworld? How successful was her "psychoanalysis"? To answer these questions, we must look closely at the six chapters that Esther narrates in the novel's final double monthly number, and we must attend more carefully than ever to the voice of Esther Woodcourt.

In posing these questions and trying to answer them, I am returning to the point in chapter 1 where I began and to two questions that I left dangling in my initial discussion of Esther's discovery of her mother's body: what does this scene leave out? and what does it do for Esther in her role as narrator?

What the scene leaves out—what Esther leaves out—is any description of her reaction, then or now, to the discovery of her mother's body. When we turn to the beginning of chapter 60, we read,

> I proceed to other passages of my narrative. From the goodness of all about me, I derived such consolation as I can never think of unmoved. I have already said so much of myself, and so much still remains, that I will not dwell upon my sorrow. I had an illness, but it was not a long one; and I would avoid even this mention of it, if I could quite keep down the recollection of their sympathy.
>
> I proceed to other passages of my narrative. (916)

I suspect that any even moderately curious reader will want to know more than Esther tells us here, both about her illness and the process of her recovery, and about the effect on her current and ongoing sense of who she is of all the new information and experience she has accumulated. Yet she describes no dreams, as she did after her previous illness, and she never again refers directly to her mother in any of the six remaining chapters that she narrates, other than to mention in passing that on one occasion when she sat with Jarndyce (but before he reveals his plan for her to marry Woodcourt) she wore "my mourning dress" (920).

By this point, readers familiar with Esther's habit of narrative indirection may be expecting that whenever she witnesses (and reexperiences) a traumatic "primal" scene such as the one at the end of chapter 59, she will displace her reaction onto a nearby figure in her narrative. Yet no convenient surrogate appears in chapters 59 or 60 to act out or give voice to her hidden feelings. Ada has her own life by now and no longer seems available for the role of doll, and Hortense has been safely spirited away by the "homely Jupiter," Inspector Bucket.

In order to find the displaced voice that fills the gap between chapters 59 and 60, we must look elsewhere in the novel, back to a scene near the very beginning of Esther's narrative in chapter 3. There Esther writes of an occasion when she had been reading aloud to Miss Barbary from the Bible and was suddenly interrupted by a loud cry.

> I was stopped by my godmother's rising, putting her hand to her head, and crying out, in an awful voice, from quite another part of the book:
>
> "Watch ye therefore! lest coming suddenly he find you sleeping. And what I say unto you, I say unto all, Watch!"
>
> In an instant, while she stood before me repeating these words, she fell down on the floor. I had no need to cry out; her voice had sounded through the house, and been heard in the street.
>
> She was laid upon her bed. For more than a week she lay there, little altered outwardly; with her old handsome resolute frown that I so well knew, carved upon her face. Many and many a time, in the day and in the night, with my head upon the pillow by her that my whispers might be plainer to her, I kissed her, thanked her, prayed for her, asked her for her blessing and forgiveness, entreated her to give me the least sign that she knew or heard me. No, no, no. Her face was immovable. To the very last, and even afterwards, her frown remained unsoftened. (32–33)

The reader who encounters this passage for the first time or who persists in reading it only as the description of an event from Esther's childhood will be discomforted, I suspect, both by the outpouring of grief it contains and by Esther's apparent attachment to the source of her early emotional abuse. The reader who comes back to this passage after having completed the novel and who keeps in mind Esther's position as retrospective narrator will find it easier to recognize in the excess of emotion here a transference, in the moment of writing, of Esther's feelings about her mother's death in chapter 59 onto the figure of the godmother. More than just the description of an event from Esther's past, the passage is itself an event in the present time of narrating. Or, to put it slightly differently, the act of enunciation—voice as registered in the *sjužet*—erupts into and inflects the utterance—the *énoncé*.

What authorizes and confirms this reading for me is the phrase that Esther uses to describe her godmother's sudden cry. She calls it "an awful voice, from quite another part of the book."[1] The "book" here is both the godmother's Bible and the book we are reading. Just as there are two books, so there are two different awful cries. One comes from the godmother, the other from the narrator. The second awful cry, with its despairing "No, no, no," belongs to Esther, and it comes from somewhere between the end of chapter 59 and the start of chapter 60. It is Esther's anguished response to her mother's death, both at the time of the event and now in the time of writing and reexperiencing it. Once again, the shift from past- into present-tense narration is a clue to the repetitive dimension of this scene as well as to its persistence "now" in the mind of Esther Woodcourt. The cry "No, no, no" has no fixed temporality. The phrase "Many and many a time, in the day and in the night" signals the recursive pattern of trauma. The immovable face, the unsoftened frown, belong both to the godmother and to Lady Dedlock, and they remain "to the very last, and *even afterwards*" (my emphasis). Esther Woodcourt is still haunted by the death of her mother. Seven years afterwards, she is still in mourning, or rather, she is still afflicted with what Freud calls melancholy.

Has Esther's "psychoanalysis" with Bucket been successful? Has the homely Orpheus successfully brought her back from the underworld? I think not. Or if he has done so in part, he has not entirely succeeded in liberating her from the ghosts of her past. Esther marries Allan Woodcourt, the man she loves, and she becomes a mother. These are undeniable signs of greater emotional strength, as is her ability to confront and reprimand Skimpole "in the gentlest words I could use" for his "disregard of several moral obligations" (933). The marriage to Woodcourt has troubled many readers, who find it sentimental and a concession, on Dickens's part, to the demands of his audience and the conventions of the marriage plot. I too find it troubling, but for other reasons.

The marriage to Woodcourt, as other critics have pointed out, is an arranged affair. Jarndyce, having abandoned his own tepid and slightly incestuous love for Esther, arrogates to himself the role of author, turns his heroine over to a worthy, if slightly wooden, surrogate of whom he approves, and sets them up in a doll's house that is the exact replica, down to its very name, of his own Bleak House. Is Esther happy with this arrangement? Yes, of course, but there is still something more than just a little artificial about the happy ending thus effected. There is too much contrivance here. The ending feels imposed rather than achieved, and this, I believe, is the reason many readers have been less than fully satisfied by it.[2] It feels more like the simulacrum of a happy ending, almost a parody, rather than the real thing, just as the second Bleak House is a simulacrum of the first rather than a genuine new home. But whom should we hold responsible for whatever is unsatisfactory in this ending? The conventional answer has been "Dickens" or "Victorian morality" or something similar. But why not lay the blame on Jarndyce and his sentimental, self-indulgent philanthropy? After all, the book never whole-heartedly endorses his generosity, which, as his indulgence of Skimpole shows, contains a large dose of self-deception. Perhaps Skimpole is right when, in his posthumous autobiography, he writes that "Jarndyce, in common with most other men I have known, is the Incarnation of Selfishness" (935).

What is most notably missing in the happy ending is any agency on Esther's part. She becomes a character in someone else's plot, not a plot of her own making. To the extent that she has significant agency in the final sections of the novel, it is her agency as narrator. Whatever her passive role in the marriage plot arranged for her, she remains the active producer not only of six final chapters but also of her retrospective narrative, written, we must remember, entirely after her marriage to Allan and addressed, not to him or to anyone she knows, but to the "unknown friend."

To answer the question of whether Esther's "psychoanalysis" has been successful, then, we must look not so much at the story she reports, the *fabula,* as at her narrative discourse and at the voice that she uses as narrator in order to tell that story. Again we are back to Esther Woodcourt. In the reading that I give to it, Esther's narrative is a marvelous ghost story. It is a narrative full of contradictory impulses, containing passages of brilliant, powerful, hallucinatory prose, equal to the best that any Victorian novelist (even Dickens!) could produce, but also replete with coy evasions, sentimental self-indulgence, and a studied, almost masochistic desire to hide her beauty, sexuality, and creativity from the view of others and from herself. To the extent that generations of readers have found her "unlikable" as a narrator, she has succeeded in this effort at concealment. My task in reading her otherwise has been to bring out the darker, more powerful and conflicted side of Esther's character and to locate the sources both of her strengths and of her neuroses, the two being closely connected. Esther's struggle to give voice to her inner conflicts and to report on her descent into dark, terrifying regions of her psyche is heroic and deserves more respect than critics have generally been willing to accord it. Esther is fully the equal in this regard of Jane Eyre, Lucy Snowe, or Catherine Earnshaw, and *Bleak House* deserves recognition as one of the great achievements in the tradition of the female gothic.

Critics have generally not been willing to listen to Esther's voice or else have listened to only one of her voices, the domestic, preferring, even when they do not acknowledge it openly, the other, more properly "Dickensian" narrator, the one who sets the fog machine going, the Megalosaurus waddling, the giant soot flakes falling, and who seems more directly engaged with social issues, condemning the inefficiency of Chancery and the neglect of the poor. Critics who take a more "political" approach to the novel tend to align Esther with dominant ideological structures and to see her marriage to Woodcourt as the conventional sign of narrative and ideological closure. Even those critics who find a satirical edge in Esther's accounts of the Jellyby, Pardiggle, and Turveydrop establishments and who see in her marriage to Allan an effort on Dickens's part to locate the happy couple outside the British class system (see, for example, Vanden Bossche) have difficulty following Esther into the depths of her nightmares or drawing connections between the novel's political and "psychological" plots. Still other critics, many of them attentive to feminist issues, see Esther as bravely struggling with Victorian gender ideologies and succeeding, more or less well, in establishing a precarious daughterly independence within patriarchal society (see, for example, Schor and Sternlieb) or else as achieving "healthy self love" through the exercise of her "will to live, to love and be loved, to want and then to have."[3] Yet these critics too tend to focus on the plot, on Esther's place in society, at the expense of her role as narrator, her place within language.

All of these views have merit, but none goes far enough, I believe, in accounting either for the depth of psychic pain that Esther confronts or for the residue of this pain in her retrospective narrative, as manifested in its weird temporality and dislocated voices. "My" Esther (and I believe Dever's as well) is more of a ghostwalker and a ghostwriter than other critics have allowed. She is also, as I hope to show in my final chapter, more closely connected than critics have generally suspected to the book's largest social, political, and historical concerns.

I have argued that in chapters 57 and 59 Esther undergoes a form of "psychoanalysis" with Bucket as her analyst and that he functions as the Orpheus who leads her back toward the land of the living where she can recover her identity as the beautiful queen Esther. I have also suggested that Bucket's therapeutic intervention is at best only a partial success. Like Eurydice, Esther sinks back into the underworld, not through any fault of Bucket (he does not "look back"), but because she is unable to get beyond the horrifying recognition, after looking into her mother's dead face, that she too is dead. The "failure" of her analysis with Bucket is most immediately evident in the flat affect and dead narrative voice of the opening of chapter 60: "I proceed to other passages of my narrative." Having come all the way back "up" to the burial ground, Esther can go no farther. She remains in mourning, for herself as well as for her mother, and she continues to lead her life and write her story under a cloud of melancholy, no matter how "happy" she forces herself to be.

Patients who experience "failure" in their analysis or who reach an impasse with their first analyst sometimes undertake a second course of treatment. Seven years into her marriage and after giving birth to two daughters, Esther Woodcourt returns to "psychoanalysis." Her second analysis is conducted under even more unorthodox conditions than the first, not in the closed carriage with Bucket at her side (recalling the physician's consulting room or the mesmerist's closet, two nineteenth-century analogs to the psychoanalyst's office). Instead, Esther undertakes analysis on her own, or if not entirely alone, then in the presence of an "unknown friend" to whom her narrative, we learn at the very end, is addressed. Her "second analysis" repeats some of the same ground as her first, but is more detailed and goes back much farther into the past, beginning in childhood and coming up to the very present. Esther's "second analysis" is her written life, the text that we read and reread together with her.

Who is this "unknown friend"? By definition, it is not Ada or Caddy or Jarndyce or Allan, since all of these are people known to her. Among the various possibilities, one is ourselves—that is, the reader of *Bleak House,* who if properly sympathetic and attuned to Esther (Esther Woodcourt, I mean), may provide her with the understanding and compassion she needs and deserves. Another possibility, one that I have already mentioned, is Esther's mother. If we look closely at the way in which she refers to the "unknown friend," is there not a hint that in writing the story of her life Esther may be reaching out toward the mother who still remains "unknown" to her, but whom she remembers fondly and by whom she hopes to be remembered in turn? "The few words that I have to add to what I have written, are soon penned; then I, and the unknown friend to whom I write, will part for ever. Not without much dear remembrance on my side. Not without some, I hope, on his or hers" (985). If, in her "first analysis" with Bucket, some of the "failure" of her treatment lay in the fact that she could not "part" with her mother, but tried to keep her alive within herself (Abraham and Torok would call this "incorporation" as opposed to "introjection"[4]), then perhaps in writing and now in concluding the story of her life, Esther is better able to separate from her mother and thus emerge from the condition of melancholy. Does not the careful inclusion of the gendered pronouns "his or *hers*" at the end of this sentence suggest the possibility that Esther imagines not just a reader of either sex but a specific female reader whom she remembers and whose "dear remembrance" she particularly desires?

One other possible candidate for the "unknown friend" is Esther herself. Her narrative may be addressed to an "unknown" part of herself that she realizes must be left behind if she is to move forward in her life. She recalls that self fondly at the same time that she bids it farewell. Read in this way, her written account would be oriented toward the future and toward the possibility of a stronger, more secure identity lying somewhere ahead of her. Of course, the "unknown friend" could be any combination or indeed all of these.

Although she bids farewell to her unknown friend at the beginning of this chapter, Esther is not done writing. There is still her final chapter to complete, the one entitled "The Close of Esther's Narrative."

(Whose voice speaks these chapter titles anyway?) The chapter conforms, on the whole, to the conventions of narrative closure predominant in contemporaneous works of fiction and autobiography with which Esther can be presumed to be familiar. She never mentions what books she reads, but we know that, as a student at Greenleaf school, she prepared herself to become a governess and "was not only instructed in everything that was taught at Greenleaf, but was very soon engaged in helping to instruct others" (39). It seems safe to assume, then, that she has read a few novels and knows how they are supposed to end: that is, with a summary of what has happened to most of the major figures who appear in earlier parts of the narrative.

"The Close of Esther's Narrative" provides such conventional summaries. We learn that Ada, now a widow, has given birth to a son named Richard and that she and Jarndyce are reconciled. We learn that Charley has married a neighboring miller. Esther even reports that when she looks up from her desk early in the summer morning (one of the very few times when she mentions her scene of writing), she can see the mill beginning to go round. (Is this mill a figure for the deadening routine of married life in which Charley and Esther and many Victorian women are caught?) We learn that Caddy works very hard to keep the Turveydrop dancing school going, her husband now being lame and unable to work and Mr. Turveydrop continuing to "exhibit his Deportment about town" (987). Esther "almost" forgets to mention one troubling detail in the apparently happy picture she tries to paint. Caddy and Prince's "poor little girl"—named Esther, we recall—is "deaf and dumb," but Esther tries to put a good face even on this misfortune. Caddy is an excellent mother, she tells us, "who learns, in her scanty intervals of leisure, innumerable deaf and dumb arts, to soften the affliction of her child" (987). Caddy's marriage, it seems, is also a mill, though its demands on female labor are more visible.

We read that Esther and Allan have added a miniature Growlery onto their house "expressly for my guardian," and as she mentions him, Esther even reports shedding a tear at the thought of Jarndyce, whom she continues to regard with "deepest love and veneration" and who acts as a father toward Ada's son and as "my husband's best and dearest friend" and "our children's darling" (988). Her praise of Jarndyce continues. Despite regarding him as "a superior being," Esther says she feels so familiar and easy with him that "I almost wonder at myself." (Who are "I" and "myself" in this sentence?) In many respects, nothing seems to have changed between the two of them. "I have never lost my old names, nor has he lost his; nor do I ever, when he is with us, sit in any other place than in my old chair at his side. Dame Trot, Dame Durden, Little Woman!—all just the same as ever; and I answer, Yes, dear guardian!—just the same" (988).

What is going on here, the modern reader wonders? Can this really be Dickens writing? If so, it is Dickens at his sentimental worst. How can he produce such treacly prose, especially after having written some of the magnificent passages that appear elsewhere in this book? He must be in a hurry to finish. Victorian readers required a happy ending, and so he gave them just what they wanted. But at what cost to the integrity of his novel! His sweet young heroines are always so insipid. What a disappointment! Where are waspish Miss Wade or Rosa Dartle or Estella when we need them?

Such reactions are understandable but, I think, misplaced. Critics seldom quote these final passages of Esther's at length, because they find them embarrassing. But wait—the prose gets even worse. I skip a few paragraphs to spare you the pain of reading them, but remember, this is Esther concluding her life story, concluding her "psychoanalysis," and finally getting around to telling us, in the present tense and not in retrospect, about herself and not about other people. This is the narrator's voice; this is Esther Woodcourt! "The people even praise Me as the doctor's wife. The people even like Me as I go about, and make so much of me that I am quite abashed. I owe it all to him, my love, my pride! They like me for his sake, as I do everything I do in life for his sake" (988–89). And then there is the closing dialogue between Allan and Esther, the final part of which I am obliged to quote in full:

> "My dear Dame Durden," said Allan, drawing my arm through his, "do you ever look in the glass?"
> "You know I do; you see me do it."
> "And don't you know that you are prettier than you ever were?"

> I did not know that; I am not certain that I know it now. But I know that my dearest little pets are very pretty, and that my darling is very beautiful, and that my husband is very handsome, and that my guardian has the brightest and most benevolent face that ever was seen; and that they can very well do without much beauty in me—even supposing—. (989)

Like many others before me, I find this ending very disturbing. The Esther whose powerful prose I most admire and whose animated voice I have been tracking though the course of her narrative is almost entirely absent here, hidden behind a coy, self-effacing gender stereotype. The angry, desiring, giddy, critical, eloquent Esther has disappeared, and we are left with Good Esther, a feeble substitute.

What has happened, I feel confident in saying, is that Esther has once again slipped back into her "old" identity, her identity as little old woman, Dame Durden, and so on. She hides behind a mask of modesty, deflects attention onto other people, and speaks in a false voice. If the prose seems strained and excessive in its praise of Jarndyce or, in passages I did not quote, of the "diviner quality" that she sees in Ada's face, now "purified" of its earlier sadness, it is because Esther is trying so hard to force a happy ending on the story she has told, an ending that the facts of the story do not always sustain. Her determined effort to impose happiness cannot prevent discordant details, such as Caddy's labor or her deaf and dumb child, from slipping through the narrative filter.

If Esther's first "psychoanalysis" with Bucket proved only partly successful in restoring her to life, her "second analysis" undertaken on her own has not produced significantly better results, at least judging from the quality of voice in these closing sections. Esther/Eurydice has once again slipped back into the underworld, not fully alive, still searching in Ada's face or in Jarndyce's or in Allan's for the look that will bring her back to life, but finding instead only "my old looks."

The only trace that remains of that other, more passionate Esther—the Esther whom I love—is the space opened up by the last word she writes and by the incomplete syntax of her final sentence. How do we understand the act of "supposing"? Dictionaries tell us that to suppose means to lay down as an assumption or hypothesis, to assume something tentatively as true for the sake of argument. More generally, it means to think speculatively, to imagine, to conjecture. To suppose (*sub+ponere*) means literally to place below or underneath; it is thus a form of mental (or perhaps vocal) displacement. We have seen Esther engaged in "supposing" on previous occasions. "If these pages contain a great deal about me, I can only *suppose* it must be because I have really something to do with them, and can't be kept out" (137). And again: "I *suppose* there is nothing Pride can so little bear with, as Pride itself, and that she was punished for her imperious manner" (299). In passages like these, to "suppose" means that Esther has begun to think more boldly and more critically. In the broadest sense, "supposing" means to consider alternate possibilities by placing something underneath what is already there.[5] A supposition is thus an underthought, a subtext. What Esther "supposes" literally in the conversation with Allan is that she may in fact be beautiful, that she may be queen Esther. The Esther who remains open to "supposing" retains at least the possibility of recovering the voice I find missing from her final chapters.[6] This Esther is not fully contained by her "old looks" or by her "Dame Durden" identity or by "The Close of Esther's Narrative."

I have said that the other, more powerful Esther is largely absent from the novel's final pages. But if she is absent, where can she have gone? The logic of my argument (and of Dever's as well) suggests that we should look for her elsewhere, not so much in the doll's house that Jarndyce has prepared for her and Allan as perhaps at Chesney Wold, near her mother's tomb. "Down in Lincolnshire," the novel's penultimate chapter, is a more fitting location for her than "The Close of Esther's Narrative." Proximity to the mother has always been the source of Esther's greatest strength.

Has Esther been able to migrate across the boundary that separates hers from the other narrative? Do we find her "Down in Lincolnshire"? I suppose we do, and I suggest that we go looking for her there.

The final, double monthly number of *Bleak House* contains four illustrations. As with the regular, single numbers, these illustrations were bound at the front of the monthly installment, after the advertisements and before the letterpress began. Two of the four illustrations were destined to take their place as part of the front matter of the novel when it was published in volume form: the frontispiece, a dark plate containing an image of Chesney Wold; and the vignette title page, showing Jo the crossing sweeper. The other two illustrations correspond to passages in the verbal text of the final number. "Magnanimous conduct of Mr. Guppy" depicts the comical scene of Guppy's second proposal of marriage to Esther in chapter 64. Stylistically it is in the familiar, more linear and caricatural manner of Phiz's earlier work.

The novel's final illustration, or at least the one that accompanies the passage closest to the end of the novel's verbal text, is "The Mausoleum at Chesney Wold" (fig. 9). This illustration, one of the novel's dark plates, corresponds to a passage near the beginning of chapter 66, "Down in Lincolnshire." The passage in question describes Lady Dedlock's final resting place in the Dedlock family mausoleum and, in particular, the regular visits faithfully paid by Sir Leicester to the site of his wife's grave.

> Up from among the fern in the hollow, and winding by the bridle-road among the trees, comes sometimes to this lonely spot the sound of horses' hoofs. Then may be seen Sir Leicester—invalided, bent, and almost blind, but of a worthy presence yet—riding with a stalwart man beside him, constant to his bridle-rein. When they come to a certain spot before the mausoleum door, Sir Leicester's accustomed horse stops of his own accord, and Sir Leicester, pulling off his hat, is still for a few moments before they ride away. (981)

Told by the unnamed, present-tense narrator, this brief paragraph moves in three sentences from a slightly spooky evocation of approaching sound to a description of the two visitors, Sir Leicester and the stalwart George, to their halt at a particular spot before the mausoleum, and finally to their departure.

The accompanying illustration depicts the scene just described. An elaborate, baroque mausoleum, surmounted by kneeling figures and a large urn, occupies the center of the image. The tomb is located in a long alley-way of trees that form a sinister canopy or arch over the architectural structure. The view is from the front, directly opposite

ENDINGS 81

FIG. 9. "The Mausoleum at Chesney Wold."

the mausoleum door. An iron fence surrounds the structure. Carved statues guard the entrance, and four stone pillars mark the boundaries of the plot. In the foreground the underbrush is low enough so as not to obscure access to the view. The overall atmosphere, enhanced by the dark shadows of the trees and the dark lineation of the plate, is decidedly gloomy. The viewpoint is presumably that of Sir Leicester and George from their horses. Although both men pause before the gravesite, it is Sir Leicester for whom this place has special meaning. He is the image's unseen internal focalizer. The focalization can be understood equally as external, as located in a heteroperceptive viewpoint. "The Mausoleum at Chesney Wold" is thus an example of what Bal calls free indirect perception.

Two details in the verbal text stand out for me: the mausoleum door and Sir Leicester's poor eyesight. The first raises issues of access to and from the crypt; the second may explain why Sir Leicester, assuming him to be the unseen internal focalizer of the illustration, does not notice the strange figure, from all appearances female, standing inside the fence and just in front of the door.[7] Who is this figure?

Not all editions of *Bleak House* show this figure clearly. In some, including both original serial parts and bound volumes of the first edition, the ink is so dark that the figure fades into the shadows. This loss of precision may in some cases be simply the result of bad inking. In others, it may be due to the fact that Dickens's publishers, Bradbury and Evans, had taken to reproducing Phiz's images using lithography, a technique in which designs were copied onto stone with a greasy material and printed impressions taken from them. In an undated letter to Dickens, Browne complained particularly of the ruinous effect that lithography had on his plates for *Bleak House*. "I am told," he writes, "that from 15 to 25,000 [copies] are monthly printed from lithographic transfers—some of these impressions, when the etching is light and sketchy, will pass muster with the uninitiated—but, the more elaborate the etching—the more villainous the transfer."[8] Browne is correct to complain and would be fully justified, in the case of a dark plate such as "The Mausoleum at Chesney Wold," in saying that "wretched printing" has ruined a subtle effect that might otherwise be visible. Whatever the reason for the considerable variation between different impressions of the mausoleum image, I confess that I take a certain pleasure at the thought that some early editions of *Bleak House* contain the strange figure standing by the mausoleum door and some do not. The figure is a ghost, and, as ghosts are wont to do, it comes and goes. Some people see the ghost, and others, like Sir Leicester, do not. Sometimes the ghost appears distinctly, and sometimes it fades into the shadows—or rather, into the ink.

From as early as chapter 2, where the view from Lady Dedlock's windows is described as "alternately a lead-coloured view, and a view in India ink" (21), ink is an important motif in the novel. (Did this passage encourage Phiz to produce so many dark plates?) Recalling her first sight of Caddy Jellyby, Esther introduces her as "a jaded, and unhealthy-looking, though by no means plain girl, at the writing table, who sat biting the feather of her pen, and staring at us. I suppose nobody was ever in such a state of ink" (53). When Guppy first appears in the narrative, Esther describes him as "a young man who had inked himself by accident" (42). Krook's rag and bottle warehouse contains "quantities of dirty bottles: blacking bottles, medicine bottles, ginger-beer and soda-water bottles, pickle bottles, wine bottles, ink bottles.... There were a great many ink bottles" (67–68).

The business of the law could not exist without vast supplies of paper, ink, and other writing materials.[9] Mr. Snagsby, Law Stationer in Cooks Court, makes his living from this trade. The narrator tells us that Snagsby "has dealt in all sorts of blank forms of legal process." Here follows a marvelous catalog of articles for sale in Snagsby's shop that is too long to quote in its entirety, but that includes "office-quills, pens, ink, India-rubber, pounce, pins, pencils, sealing-wax, and wafers;... red tape, and green ferret;... string boxes, rulers, inkstands—glass and leaden, penknives, scissors, bodkins, and other small office-cutlery" (154). The passage continues with an explanation of how it happens that Snagsby's shop bears the name "PEFFER and SNAGSBY," since Peffer is now dead, and it concludes with a fanciful account of the return of Snagsby's former business partner's ghost—one of the many ghosts in this book and one closely connected to the business of paper and ink.

Ink is everywhere in *Bleak House*. Tulkinghorn toys with inkstand tops as he tries to solve the mystery of Lady Dedlock's reaction to seeing Nemo's handwriting. Nemo of course is a copyist, and when we are first introduced to the room in which he died, the narrator describes it as "a wilderness marked with a rain of ink" (164). The novel is full of letters and legal documents, all written by hand and all in ink. Caddy's deaf and dumb baby is born with "curious little dark veins in its face, and curious little dark marks under its eyes, like faint remembrances of poor Caddy's inky days" (768). Even Jo, though excluded from legal process and from all forms of writing, bears traces of ink in his speech. For him the inquest is an "Inkwhich" (260), and he frequently declares, "*I* don't know nothink!" (264). To be stained with ink in this book is dangerous. Esther too, we recall, is a writer, and though she scarcely ever mentions her writing implements, she too must occasionally carry the signs of her inky involvement. At the beginning of the chapter in which she reports being taken ill, she tries to teach her maid Charley to write. In Charley's hand, however, "every pen appeared to become perversely animated, and to go wrong and crooked, and to stop, and splash and sidle into corners, like a saddle donkey" (486). Is it too much to suggest that ink may be a figure for the disease that passes from the graveyard where the law-writer's corpse is buried to Jo and then to Charley, whom Esther nurses, and finally to Esther herself?

I have indulged myself with this digression on the subject of ink in order to prepare the way for a consideration of the inky figure in "The Mausoleum at Chesney Wold." I believe the figure is a ghost, something that no previous critic or commentator on the novel to my knowledge seems to have noticed. But whose ghost would it be? Certainly the family ghost, the ghost of the first Lady Dedlock in the story told by Mrs. Rouncewell in chapter 7, but also the ghost of the most recent Lady Dedlock, risen here to greet Sir Leicester though he cannot see her.

The ghost is also Esther, I believe, not in her incarnation as "Good Esther," the disappointing heroine of the marriage plot, but the darker, ghostwalking and ghostwriting Esther whose advocate I have tried throughout this essay to be. Moreover—and here I'm just supposing—I think that Esther is the unseen internal focalizer of this scene. She is the one who sees the ghost, or rather, since she *is* the ghost, she here watches her own ghostly emanation from her ghostly retrospective viewpoint.[10] Sir Leicester does not see the ghost, and there is no indication in the verbal text that the other narrator has noted it either. Perhaps the unseen external focalizer shares her vision in free indirect perception, but there is no way we can be sure of this. In any event, if these speculations have merit, there is reason to believe that Esther—or a part of her—has fled from her constricted identity as the doctor's wife, has migrated across the boundary separating her from the other narrative, and has joined her mother "*down* in Lincolnshire." "Down" and "up" indicate crucial spatial locations in the novel, intrapsychic as well as on the map of England. Esther seems capable of being in more than one place at the same time.

Bleak House has many endings. It is also a novel that refuses to end. A multiplot novel, it contains endings to many of its minor subplots. Richard dies, Charley marries, Tulkinghorn is murdered, Jarndyce and Jarndyce gets consumed in costs, George visits his brother and goes to live in the Keeper's lodge at Chesney Wold. Even the Bagnets and Mrs. Rouncewell and Sir Leicester's debilitated cousin make brief final appearances. The book's major plots have their endings too. One is at the end of monthly number 18, when Esther discovers her mother's body. Another is at the end of the final monthly number, "The Close of Esther's Narrative," where Esther retreats to her role as Dame Durden, but leaves open the possibility of "supposing—." Yet another is the book's final illustration, "The Mausoleum at Chesney Wold," which shows us that the family ghost continues to walk. Another ending, the last that I will consider, is the novel's penultimate chapter, "Down in Lincolnshire," which is the final chapter told by the unnamed present-tense narrator.

The principal figures in this chapter are architectural, first the mausoleum (with its illustration) and finally Chesney Wold itself (pictured in the frontispiece). A synecdoche for the nation as a whole (the Bleak House of the novel's title), Chesney Wold is a haunted house. Its resident ghost, however, turns out most delightfully to be Volumnia, Sir Leicester's antiquated cousin, who occupies the otherwise empty house and "holds even the dragon Boredom at bay" (983). Whereas the mausoleum remains a place of gloom, Chesney Wold, by contrast, is occasionally transformed into a place of ghostly gaiety. In a lengthy paragraph that describes Volumnia's delight in the occasional country dances held in a neighboring assembly room, the narrator describes how Volumnia, "a tuckered sylph...in fairy form," skips about with "girlish vivacity" as she did long ago in her youth.

> Then does she twirl and twine, a pastoral nymph of good family, through the mazes of the dance. Then do the swains appear with tea, with lemonade, with sandwiches, with homage. [Notice the playful zeugma here!] Then is she kind and cruel, stately and unassuming, various, beautifully wilful. Then is there a singular kind of parallel between her and the little glass chandeliers of another age, embellishing that assembly-room; which, with their meagre stems, their spare little drops, their disappointing knobs where no drops are, their bare little stalks from which knobs and drops have both departed, and their little feeble prismatic twinkling, all seem Volumnias. (984)

It is a comic *danse macabre,* at once ludicrous and grotesque—a grim emblem of mortality, but also a reminder that ghosts are sometimes funny. The final image of the chandelier, with its multiple reflections of Volumnia in prismatic stems and "drops" (recalling the Ghost's Walk refrain, "drip, drip, drip," as well as Esther's parting "thaw-drop" kiss at Windsor), is a fitting image for the novel as a whole, in which every female figure seems somehow the ghostly refraction of Esther and her mother.

5

WHERE IS DICKENS IN ALL THIS? DOES *BLEAK HOUSE* CONTAIN any reflections, ghostly or otherwise, of its author? In addition to exercising extraordinary craft in the creation of its female first-person narrator, does Dickens enter in any way into the fictional world of his novel? Thus far, I have studiously tried to keep him out of my critical discourse, carefully attributing all the language and narration in the novel either to Esther Woodcourt or to "the unnamed present-tense narrator." I even went out of my way to argue against attributing the illustrations to Phiz/Dickens, substituting instead the concept of focalization in order to be able to assign the viewpoint in these images either to a character, usually Esther, or to an unseen external focalizer. Such methodological restraint has certain advantages, especially for an approach interested in narrative voice. Moreover, it allows me to skirt the vexing questions of intentionality and purpose that accompany the concept of the "author."

But can we keep Dickens out entirely, and do we really want to? In this respect we might do well to reconsider something that Esther writes early in her narrative. She says (and I can imagine Dickens smiling to himself as he penned these words): "I hope any one who may read what I write, will understand that if these pages contain a great deal about me, I can only suppose it must be because I have really something to do with them, and can't be kept out." Rather than continue trying to keep him out, I propose to open my methodological door and let Dickens back in. Or, to adopt the chandelier metaphor from the end of chapter 66, I suggest that we think of the novel as a great assembly room whose mirrors reflect or refract innumerable images of Dickens.

Before attempting to pursue the notion of *Bleak House* as a giant hall of Dickensian mirrors, it is useful to recall that Dickens began writing the novel in November 1851 (his earliest mention of the idea for a new novel dates from February of that year) and that it was published serially between March 1852 and September 1853. The novel that immediately preceded it was *David Copperfield* (1849–50), Dickens's most autobiographical novel and one that incorporates almost word for word several passages from the autobiographical document that Dickens wrote sometime in the late 1840s and showed to his friend and literary advisor, John Forster. This "autobiographical fragment," as it has come to be known, contains the story of Dickens's time at the blacking factory when he was a young boy, an experience that some critics have treated as Dickens's childhood "trauma," one that left traces, inadvertent as well as deliberate, in many of his writings. *Copperfield* and *Bleak House* thus both belong to what some critics have called the period of Dickens's "autobiographical crisis," when he began to look more closely into hidden or secret aspects of his past and to write more frequently about childhood, both his own and that of his characters.

Dickens continued his interest in autobiographical writing throughout the period when he was composing *Bleak House*. As the editors of his letters point out, among the more than one hundred articles and stories that he published in his new journal, *Household Words,* between 1850 and 1852 (a few collaboratively written with Wills and Morley), many are autobiographical (*Letters,* 6: viii). These include "A Child's Dream of a Star," "Lying Awake," "Our School," and several other items collected in *Reprinted Pieces.* The autobiographical impulse continued strong during 1853 in such essays as "Where We Stopped Growing" and "Gone Astray." Dickens's interest in childhood had begun as early as *Oliver Twist* (some would even say with Mr. Pickwick, that elderly child), but became increasingly prominent in *Dombey and Son* (1846–48), the autobiographical fragment, the Christmas stories of the 1840s, *Copperfield*, and *Bleak House*.

In all of these texts, but especially in *David Copperfield* and in "The Haunted Man," his Christmas story of 1848, Dickens shows a keen interest in questions of memory. In her brilliant study *Knowing Dickens*, Rosemarie Bodenheimer has discussed many of the rich and complex ways in which Dickens explored the theme of memory in his writings as well as the likelihood that he was influenced by the work of Dr. John Elliotson and other Victorian scientists who wrote about dreams, states of double consciousness, and the phenomenon of what we might now call implicit or "procedural" memory.[1] Dickens had long been interested in the subject of infant memory, in the possibility that children as well as adults retain memory traces from their earliest moments of life. In *Oliver Twist,* for example, when Oliver sees the portrait of a young woman hanging on the wall in Mr. Brownlow's home, he experiences the sensation of having seen her face before, and he associates it with a memory or fantasy of his mother, who died when he was born. I mention this example in order to show that the much more sophisticated treatment of infant memory in *Bleak House*—Esther's fantasy or memory of her mother's face, "the first thing in the world I had ever seen"—is neither a critical anachronism nor an imposition on my part. Similar hints of infant memory are present in the case of little Paul Dombey, who mingles memories of his mother, also dead in childbirth, with the figure of his sister Florence and who yearns to return to the maternal "waves" where the spirit of his mother seems to reside and beckon to him.

David Copperfield is especially rich in scenes and passages suggestive of infantile memory. The first four paragraphs of chapter 2 of the novel read as follows:

> The first objects that assume a distinct presence before me, as I look far back, into the blank of my infancy, are my mother with her pretty hair and youthful shape, and Peggotty with no shape at all, and eyes so dark that they seemed to darken their whole neighbourhood in her face, and cheeks and arms

so hard and red that I wondered the birds didn't peck her in preference to apples.

I believe I can remember these two at a little distance apart, dwarfed to my sight by stooping down or kneeling on the floor, and I going unsteadily from the one to the other. I have an impression on my mind which I cannot distinguish from actual remembrance, of the touch of Peggotty's forefinger as she used to hold it out to me, and of its being roughened by needlework, like a pocket nutmeg-grater.

This may be fancy, though I think the memory of most of us can go farther back into such times than many of us suppose; just as I believe the power of observation in numbers of very young children to be quite wonderful for its closeness and accuracy. Indeed, I think that most grown men who are remarkable in this respect, may with greater propriety be said not to have lost the faculty, than to have acquired it; the rather, as I generally observe such men to retain a certain freshness, and gentleness, and capacity of being pleased, which are also an inheritance they have preserved from their childhood.

I might have a misgiving that I am "meandering" in stopping to say this, but that it brings me to remark that I build these conclusions, in part upon my own experience of myself; and if it should appear from anything I may set down in this narrative that I was a child of close observation, or that as a man I have a strong memory of my childhood, I undoubtedly lay claim to both of these characteristics.[2]

This is as close as Dickens ever comes to presenting a systematic theory of infant memory. David both articulates the theory and gives examples of it from his own life. The fact that he remembers his mother as having a "pretty face and youthful figure" and Peggotty as having "no shape at all" can be understood as indicating two different kinds of memory: one visual and thus corresponding to a later period of infancy when the baby has separated from the mother and perceives her distinctly as an "other"; and an earlier memory, tactile rather than visual and corresponding to a time when the baby still experiences the mother as undifferentiated, as part of itself.

Other details that David reports both here and later in this chapter—Peggotty's apple cheeks and arms and her nutmeg-grater forefinger (as well as the pink image of St. Paul's on her sewing workbox, the little bit of wax she uses to thread her needle, and the buttons that explode from the back of her dress whenever she embraces him and that he imagines he could follow and consume like cakes to find his way back home again, like the children in the nursery story)—all these are memory traces of the mother's breast and nipple. David has two mothers, both conveniently named Clara, and he understandably confuses them. Or rather, he has two memories of a single mother, a tactile memory from the time when he was still nursing at the breast and a visual memory from the time after he was weaned. Later, in chapter 10, when he comes home from school and walks in on the scene of his mother nursing his newborn baby brother, David even has the experience of seeing himself at his mother's breast. The accompanying illustration by Phiz, like all of the illustrations in *David Copperfield*, should be understood as focalized retrospectively by the unseen adult David who narrates the novel. In this illustration he sees himself seeing himself as his infant brother.

These examples are meant to show that Dickens, little Paul, David, and Esther Woodcourt all have in common an interest in and a shared experience of memories that arise spontaneously from the earliest moments of life and that recur, often unbidden, in ways that enrich and complicate their sense of identity and temporal location. "Impressions," "remembrances," and "fancies" are difficult for David to distinguish one from the other, but both he and Dickens seem to believe that having a "strong memory of [one's] childhood" is an asset for the novelist as well as a sign of "freshness and gentleness" in the character of anyone so endowed.

Dickens looked in the mirror daily when he shaved.[3] He also looked in the mirror when he wrote, as the well-known account of his writing practice by his daughter Mamie shows. Compelled by illness to stay at home from school one day, the young girl was allowed to remain in her father's study and observe him as he wrote. She describes him jumping from his chair and running to a mirror where he made extraordinary facial contortions, muttered to himself, and then ran back to his desk to resume writing.[4] Mamie's account suggests that Dickens literally saw the characters he describes, saw them *as himself* and even acted them out in the privacy of his study before setting them down on paper. Esther Summerson regularly looks in the mirror, and what she sees is often equally strange. Esther Woodcourt also looks in the mirror, the mirror of her younger self and the mirrors provided by the faces of people she remembers: her mother, Ada, Caddy, Charley, her godmother, Bucket—the list is long. What did Dickens see when he looked in the mirror—the mirror of his characters as well as the mirror in his study? Esther is a writer; Dickens too. What else might they have in common?

Bleak House is full of Dickensian self-reference. These references range from sly little jokes, intended probably for Forster and no one else, to allusions to Dickens's family and friends, to the evocation of places and experiences in his recent as well as distant past. Many of these seem deliberate; others may be unconscious. As Bodenheimer demonstrates, what Dickens knew is never easy to determine. The self-referential quality of the novel also extends to passages that today one might call metafictional, allusions by the novel to itself and to its own process of composition and consumption.

One set of Dickensian self-references is easy to identify. These consist of the characters who are presumably taken from "originals" whom Dickens knew about or knew personally. Thus, Skimpole is based on Leigh Hunt, Bucket on Inspector Field, Boythorn on Walter Savage Landor, Mrs. Jellyby on Caroline Chisholm, Hortense on Maria Manning, and Mrs. Rouncewell on Dickens's grandmother, who was the housekeeper on a large country estate.[5] Biographical "sources" have been proposed for various other characters in the book. Esther may recall certain aspects of Georgina Hogarth. Tulkinghorn may derive in some distant way from Forster, who was a lawyer and a bachelor and who had chambers at Lincoln's Inn Fields. Tulkinghorn's room, with its painted figure of Allegory, is taken from Forster's own quarters. The descriptions of Chesney Wold are based in part on Rockingham Castle, the estate of the Honourable Mr. and Mrs. Richard Watson, whom

Dickens visited in 1849 and again in 1851, and to whom he dedicated *David Copperfield* in 1850. And so on. Such identifications are the standard fare of old-style biographical criticism. The problem with them is not that they are wrong or uninteresting, but that they do not go far enough. There is often more than one biographical "source" for characters in the novel; another source, or one of them, is just as likely as not to be Dickens himself.

Take Skimpole, for example. Irresponsible parent, detestable parasite on the benevolence of Jarndyce, vicious betrayer of Jo to the police, in any summary of the novel's moral judgments Skimpole has to be one of the book's "villains." And yet Dickens allows him to pursue his Skimpolean performance to the end, lighthearted and blithely indifferent to Esther's prudent scolding. Skimpole's act consists of pretending that he is nothing but a child, ignorant of the world's ways, especially when it comes to money, and hence deserving of the world's unstinting generosity. Looked at from a different angle, is it not possible to see in Skimpole's impersonation of innocence something like a wish-fulfillment fantasy on Dickens's part of what it would be like to live without responsibilities, without having to be a sober, responsible Victorian public man—a man something like the upright John Jarndyce or like Dickens himself? In fact, why not make Jarndyce responsible for supporting Skimpole—Jarndyce with his dutiful but boring commitment to doing good and his endless supply (again like Dickens!) of begging letters to answer? Besides, Skimpole is an artist (like Dickens), a poet and musician, who believes that he deserves the patronage of the Victorian public.

Moreover, what is Skimpole's act if not the exaggerated version of a role that Paul Dombey, David Copperfield, and Dickens had all successfully performed, that of the Romantic child? When we look more closely at the memoir that Skimpole leaves behind for posthumous publication, it looks strangely familiar. Esther writes that Skimpole "died some five years afterwards, and left a diary behind him, with letters and other materials towards his Life; which was published, and which showed him to have been the victim of a combination on the part of mankind against an amiable child" (935). Is this not a description of the autobiographical fragment and of Dickens's motives in giving it to Forster—and of what actually happened after Dickens's death in 1870? Forster incorporated the fragment into his life of Dickens, and subsequent generations of readers have taken it seriously as the account of a sensitive, creative, amiable boy who was the "victim of a combination on the part of mankind." By the time of *Bleak House*, however, Dickens had recognized the degree of self-pity and inauthenticity in this self-representation, and he parodied it, no doubt to Forster's delight (we must remember that in 1853 no one but Forster had read the autobiographical fragment), in Skimpole's performance of the Romantic child. Skimpole deconstructs the whole notion of Romantic childhood on which figures like Paul Dombey and David Copperfield depend. In addition, Skimpole's memoir, read with the proper amount of irony, provides us with a clue as to how we might interpret *David Copperfield*—that is, as the story of an older man, a novelist like Dickens, who persuades himself and others that he was an abused and neglected child, victimized by the likes of Murdstone, Heep, and a succession of waiters, servants, and other lower-class figures (but not the kindly Peggottys) and whose self-satisfied worldly success in no way results from unkind or unethical actions on his part. Both as character and as narrator, David successfully hides behind a mask of innocence; no Esther comes along to question this pose or chastise him for irresponsibility, unless it is Heep or, somewhat earlier, Miss Mowcher. The only criticism that he is willing in retrospect to accept is Aunt Betsey's repeated charge that he was "blind, blind, blind" in not recognizing Agnes as his true soul mate. But if we look beyond his pretense of innocence, we can see that David has betrayed Emily and the Peggottys, just as he betrayed Mr. Mell at Creakle's school, and for the same reason—to curry favor with his upper-class male friend, Steerforth.[6] The difference between Skimpole and David is that David does not know that he is performing, whereas Skimpole probably does, though we can never be sure. He may be another of Dickens's great hypocrites like Pecksniff or Chadband who are so accomplished that they believe in their own performance. David's hypocrisy is not so flamboyant as Skimpole's, but it is no less insidious. The wonderful thing about *Copperfield* as a novel, and part of what makes it endlessly fascinating, is that it can be read simultaneously as one of the supreme achievements in the literature of Romantic childhood and as a critique of that tradition.

Inspector Bucket is another avatar of the author. Based without doubt on Dickens's experiences with Inspector Charles Field of the Detective Police, Bucket also reflects aspects of his creator. Like Skimpole, he is an artist with a strongly developed aesthetic sense. As he closes in on a solution to the murder of Tulkinghorn, he stands back from his work and makes an admiring professional judgment: "It is a beautiful case," he tells Sir Leicester, "—a beautiful case—and what little is wanting to complete it, I expect to be able to supply in a few hours" (811). Like the novelist admiring his own handiwork, Bucket recognizes a good job when he sees it.

Like Dickens, Bucket is a vocalist with a fondness for popular ballads. Along with Little Swills, the novel's other comic vocalist, Bucket, like Dickens, is adept in pitching his voice to different situations and audiences. He is a master of rhetoric, able to converse easily with people of all social classes and quick to work his way into their confidence. His own social background is indeterminate, though he is clearly not a member of the upper classes. As a professional, he moves comfortably from one setting to another, sometimes appearing, as if out of thin air, like some "third person" (355)—that is, like the narrator of a novel. He is endowed with certain magical or mythical attributes: a potent forefinger that he uses as a probe, a magical stick whose touch is sufficient to make young policemen "evaporate" (358). His mental capacities verge on the supernatural—or the novelistic. He "dips down to the bottom of his mind" (355) on one occasion and "mounts a high tower in his mind" (864) on another. On such occasions, he seems more like an "omniscient" narrator than a character in the story.

Bucket is the book's chief resident poet, a homely Orpheus in the mythic pattern I discussed in chapter 3. In his role as proto-psychoanalyst, descending into the depths of Esther's unconscious mind, he recalls Dickens's involvement in mesmerism and the mesmeric experiments he carried out with Madame de la Rue in Genoa and with Catherine and Georgina during the early 1840s. As Fred Kaplan has argued, mesmerism was the mid-nineteenth century's closest analog to the treatment methods developed by Freud and others at the end of the century, and Dickens was an avid practitioner of mesmeric arts. The "crystallised snow" (884) that Esther notices in Bucket's hair and eyelashes at the moment when he recognizes that Lady Dedlock and Jenny have switched clothes is a version of the crystal or mirror that the mesmerist uses to induce a trance.[7] Bucket's public persona is cheerful and confident. He seems always to be in control of any situation, but there are hints that he has known sadness in the past. He wears a "great mourning ring on his little finger" (358), again recalling Dickens, who wore a ring that he took from the hand of Mary Hogarth, his cherished sister-in-law, after her sudden death in 1837.

Bucket's novelistic and supernatural qualities belong to a larger pattern of self-referentiality in the novel. *Bleak House* is full of writers of one kind or another, and, as various commentators have noted, it is a book full of paper and documents. The novel is not only a document about the interpretation of documents, as Hillis Miller famously argued.[8] It is also, in the most literal sense, a big bundle of paper that is about the production and consumption of even more bundles of paper. One of the novel's most amusing moments of self-referentiality concerns the ending of the case of Jarndyce and Jarndyce. From early on, the novel contains joking references to the fact that it will be a very long text. The waddling Megalosaurus of the book's opening paragraph is one such allusion. Later in the same chapter we read that the case "still drags its dreary length before the Court, perennially hopeless" (17). The modern reader, faced with a text of more than 900 pages, must occasionally share the sense that *Bleak House,* like Jarndyce and Jarndyce, is interminable. But the case does come to an end, consumed with costs, and when it ends, the conclusion is a cause for popular rejoicing. Esther describes the end of the suit as follows:

> The people came streaming out [from the court] looking flushed and hot, and bringing a quantity of bad air with them. Still they were all exceedingly amused, and were more like people coming out from a Farce or a Juggler than from a court of Justice.... Presently great bundles of papers began to be carried out—bundles in bags, bundles too large to be got into

any bags, immense masses of paper of all shapes and no shapes, which the bearers staggered under, and threw down for the time being, anyhow, on the Hall pavement, while they went back to bring out more. Even these clerks were laughing. (973–74)

Anticipating the end of the novel, which has only a few more pages of its final bundle of paper remaining, the case comes to an end with bundles and bundles of waste paper, but not without producing merriment for its audience, who leave, just as Dickens hopes his readers will depart, laughing and smiling.

All the jokes about ink are part of the novel's pattern of metafictional self-reference. To be "in Chancery" usually means to be stained somehow by ink. Ink is an analog of disease, the fever that moves invisibly across society and leaves its mark on people's bodies, sometimes killing them, as it does Richard. Ink stains also have another, more personal significance for Dickens. They recall his time at Warren's Blacking factory. Ink stains not only suggest one of the minor occupational hazards of being a professional writer; they also allude to a secret from Dickens's past. It should not surprise us that blacking bottles and ink bottles show up together in Krook's "Rag and Bottle Warehouse" (67). Even the word "warehouse" echoes one of the terms Dickens uses in the autobiographical fragment to identify Warren's Blacking.

It is worth recalling once again that, when the novel first appeared, only Dickens and Forster would have understood the references to blacking bottles. The blacking references function like a secret code between the two men, a set of inside jokes that only they could share. Making Tulkinghorn the novel's chief villain, putting him in Forster's rooms, and then killing him is another form of private joke between the two friends, as is the sly reference to Forster's secret erotic life: the bachelor lawyer who likes pretty women and who would eventually in 1856 marry a rich widow many years his junior. One could even speculate that Forster is "the unknown friend" to whom Dickens writes, a friend "unknown" to other readers of the book, though not, of course, to its author.

Most of the autobiographical references I have considered thus far are relatively lighthearted and playful in tone, and there are others in more or less the same vein. Mr. Guppy, for example, is no doubt an exaggerated and gently self-mocking portrait of the artist as a young man during his years as a brash young law clerk in the firm of Ellis and Blackmore. Dickens's fondness for Guppy is evident; despite his annoying attentions to Esther and his half-hearted blackmail attempt with Lady Dedlock, he is basically good-hearted and in the end even willing to stand up to Tulkinghorn in order to keep his word to Esther. As a reward, he gets to appear in more illustrations than any other minor character in the book and has his own comic exit scene in which he repeats his earlier marriage proposal to Esther. Dickens likes Guppy, and so do we.

Bleak House contains other autobiographical elements, however, that are much less playful in tone. Not surprisingly, these have more to do with the Esther plot than with the comic or metafictional dimensions of the book, and they partake of the more somber, ghostly quality that I have discussed in relation to the Esther narrative. Before proceeding along what will be a much darker and more speculative path of inquiry, I want to make clear both what I am trying and what I am not trying to do. In considering parallels between Dickens's life and elements in the story of Esther Summerson, I am not trying to privilege biography at the expense of fiction or to argue that Dickens's "life" is the source of the fictional representations we find in the novel. Rather, I am attempting something more modest—a juxtaposition of patterns that I see in the available documents about Dickens's life and similar patterns in the document called *Bleak House*. I do not give precedence to one bundle of papers over the other. Both are texts, and the juxtaposition may help to shed light on the fictionality of the so-called life and on previously unrecognized personal dimensions in the fiction—perhaps also on a mutually constitutive dynamic between the two.

I take my cue here from Rosemarie Bodenheimer, whose admirable study of Dickens's fiction in relation to his letters might be considered an example and possible model of a "new biographical criticism," by analogy to the "new historicism" of recent decades. Bodenheimer's approach (some might call it a methodology, though the term implies a more systematic practice than seems appropriate) is to explore certain crucial issues in Dickens's moral and emotional life, focusing on recurring themes and patterns that cut across the different forms of writing, but without attempting to produce either a full biographical narrative or a complete critical reading of any single work. In so doing, she avoids the "straight jacket," as she calls it, of biography, which remains tied to chronology and which tends to privilege the "life" as source and cause of the writing, as well as the obligation to treat novels or stories as organic wholes that ask to be read and discussed in their entirety.

As she explains concisely in her introduction, her approach is not to negotiate "between 'the life' and 'the work,' or what we might now call the lost 'real' and the textual imaginary." For her this is an untenable distinction, since there is no "life," only another set of texts on which speculation and interpretation must be based. Her approach, rather, is to set these different texts in play, to read them alongside each other without privileging one over the other, and to "make connections and interpretive suggestions."[9] In the final part of this chapter I hope to do something similar.

On August 16, 1850, Catherine Dickens gave birth to a daughter, her ninth child. As was his custom with all his children, Dickens gave the child its name. He called the baby Dora Annie, after two of the female characters in the novel he was completing at the time. Dora, we recall, is David Copperfield's "child wife"; Annie is Annie Strong, Dr. Strong's young wife, who is suspected of infidelity, but who turns out to be of good character after all. In the course of the novel, in sections that Dickens had planned but not yet written, Dora dies. Before dying, however, she had become pregnant and, in chapter 48, has either a miscarriage or a stillborn baby. During the latter part of August 1850, Dickens was immersed in finishing monthly number 17 of *Copperfield*. On August 16, the day of Dora's birth, he left London for Broadstairs, where he planned to complete his monthly number. With him went Georgina and the other children: Charley, Mamie, Katey, Walter, Frank, Alfred, and Sydney. Catherine remained in London with her mother and the baby. Henry, the youngest (age 2), may have stayed with his mother.

On August 17, Dickens wrote to Catherine from Broadstairs to give her the family news and to report on his progress with *Copperfield*. The letter is full of little jokes, mostly about the children and their reactions to the birth of their new little sister, but there is an odd undercurrent of comment about the baby. "Upon the whole," Dickens writes, "I think the baby rather a failure down here." He goes on to say that Charley, the oldest son, "was the most struck last night as connecting it [the baby] with you." Sydney, he goes on, "has been the most reflective on the subject to-day." What follows is Dickens's playful explanation of why the baby is considered a "failure." Sydney asks, "I say Pa, can Dora talk?" When given the answer no, Sydney "seemed to think that weak on her part and put the question, 'Is she tall?'" Dickens then measures off "about a quarter of a yard on the table." Sydney, unimpressed, "gave her up after that" (*Letters*, 6: 150). The rest of the letter is cheerful and full of local gossip. Dickens reports that he has made no further progress with *Copperfield* and that he does not know when he will see Catherine again. "Of course I shall see you next week as soon as I can possibly finish the No. concerning which I am rather low and penitent to-night, but shall brush up" (6: 151).

On August 20, four days after his new daughter's birth, Dickens wrote to Forster, again from Broadstairs, "I have been very hard at work these three days, and have still Dora to kill. But with good luck, I may do it to-morrow" (6: 153). On the same Tuesday, writing again to Catherine, Dickens reports that he has been working "nine hours at a stretch today, and did the same yesterday." He continues, "I am not sure whether I shall be able to get to town on Thursday, or whether I shall not finish until that evening, and be prevented from coming until Friday. It depends upon Dora—I mean *my* Dora." The letter concludes with an expression of pleasure at the news, in a letter received from Catherine's mother, that she is doing well. "I am quite delighted, and can stick to my work bravely, hearing such excellent accounts of you" (6: 152).

On the following day, writing once more to Catherine, he speaks again of his work and of his travel plans: "Even now, I am uncertain of my movements, for, after another splitting day, I still have Dora to kill—I mean the Copperfield Dora—and cannot make certain how long it will take to do." Once again, the date of his return to London gets pushed back. "If I can't come tomorrow, I shall come on Friday, when I have a good deal before me at the H.W. office. I shall not come back until Saturday morning in any case. And of course come when I may, I shall come straight home" (6: 153). We can only surmise as to Catherine's reaction to this sequence of events—the separation from her older children and her sister, her husband's absence and uncertain date of return, the news of her baby's "failure" with the other children, and Dickens's repeated joking references to "killing" Dora.

In the months following her birth, Dora did not thrive. On February 3, Dickens wrote to Mrs. Leech to say that "our poor little Dora is very ill—with something like congestion of the Brain" (6: 280). So concerned were he and Catherine that they hastened to have the baby baptized at home by the Reverend White, who was dining with them at Devonshire Terrace. A few days later, in a letter to her friend Miss Greville, Georgina reports that "my sister's little baby . . . is recovering nicely though still very weak" (6: 284, n3). At any rate, Dora was well enough for Dickens to have her brought down to the *Household Words* office on March 26 to visit him. Why a baby only seven months old should be brought to her father's workplace will become clearer in a moment.

If the baby seemed to be getting stronger, the mother was not doing well. Sometime in the early months of 1851, Catherine became ill. We have few details of her illness, but it seems clear that she was suffering from nervous depression, perhaps of a postpartum variety. Dickens first consulted his friend Dr. Southwood Smith, who expressed serious concern about her condition. On March 8, Dickens wrote to Dr. James Wilson, a physician to whom he had been introduced by his friend Bulwer Lytton: "I am anxious to place Mrs. Dickens under your care. As her case is a nervous one and of a peculiar kind, I forbear to describe it, or to state what Dr. Southwood Smith has particularly requested me to mention to you, as rendering great caution necessary, until I have the pleasure of seeing you" (6: 309). Wilson was a hydropathic practitioner in Malvern, 140 miles to the northwest of London. He had treated Bulwer Lytton with success and, later in the year, would also treat Carlyle. In the letter to Wilson, Dickens makes arrangements for Catherine to be sent to Malvern, accompanied by her maid Anne Brown, to undergo the water cure under Wilson's supervision.

The following day, in a letter to Mrs. Watson, Dickens gives a few more details about Kate's condition and the cure that awaited her in Malvern. "I am rather uneasy about Kate, who has an alarming disposition of blood to the head, attended with giddiness and dimness of sight. I am inclined to believe that it is not at all a new disorder with her. After taking the most sensible advice I could get (including my own) I have resolved to carry her down to Malvern, and put her under rigorous discipline of exercise, air, and cold water" (6: 311). All the while during this family crisis, which required him to travel back and forth by train between London and Malvern, Dickens maintained his usual busy schedule of activities, overseeing the work at *Household Words,* advising Miss Coutts about her philanthropic projects, doing some writing and editing of his own, speaking publicly on various subjects, and preparing for an elaborate amateur theatrical production of Bulwer Lytton's five-act comedy *Not So Bad as We Seem; or, Many Sides to a Character,* to be performed under his direction at the Duke of Devonshire's home before an audience that was to include the queen and members of her court.

He had finished writing *Copperfield* the previous October. As usual on the occasion of completing a novel, his feelings were a mixture of pleasure and regret. "Oh, my dear Forster," he wrote on October 21, "if I were to say half of what *Copperfield* makes me feel tonight, how strangely, even to you, I should be turned inside-out! I seem to be sending some part of myself into the Shadowy World" (6: 195). His use of the phrase "the Shadowy World" is of special interest. For Dickens, the "shadowy world" was a complex, fertile, and mysterious zone, at once the end and the source of life—a realm of death and ghostliness, but also the prenatal oceanic world from which babies come, trailing Wordsworthian clouds of glory. The shadowy world was also the realm of the unconscious and the source of creativity. The fallow period between his novels was often for Dickens a time of unusual activity—of travel, amateur theatricals, journalism, and public speaking. It was also a period of gestation when ideas for new novels came to him from the "shadowy world." He first mentions the idea that would eventually form the basis for his next novel in a letter to Mary Boyle on February 21, 1851. In this letter he refers to "the first shadows of a new story hovering in a ghostly way about me (as they usually begin to do, when I have finished an old one)" (6: 298). From the beginning, *Bleak House* seems to have been a ghost story.

While Kate remained at Malvern, Dickens threw himself frenetically into the preparations for Bulwer's play, revising the manuscript, recruiting actors, arranging for the scenery, organizing rehearsals, and writing letters to various correspondents in connection with the production. In addition to directing, he would play the leading role himself. In the midst of all this activity, on March 25, his father, John, was taken ill with an infection of the bladder and was obliged to undergo without chloroform what Dickens calls "the most terrible operation known in surgery" (6: 333). On March 31 John Dickens died. Dickens was at his father's bedside. With him were his mother, Elizabeth, his brothers Alfred and Augustus, his sister Letitia, and her husband, Henry Austin. Also present were Mrs. Elizabeth Smithson (widow of Charles) and her sister Amelia Thompson, who had come to help in this emergency, as Dickens had done on Charles Smithson's death in 1844.

After his father's funeral, Dickens resumed preparations for the play, continuing to shuttle back and forth between London and Malvern when he could. Meanwhile, Dora's health remained precarious. On April 15 he was scheduled to deliver a speech at the sixth annual Dinner of the Theatrical Fund, held in the London Tavern. According to Forster, efforts to postpone and reschedule the dinner to a later date proved unsuccessful. Dickens left his daughter's bedside to attend the dinner. "I had been nursing her, before I went out," he later wrote to Henry Austin (6: 352). At the dinner, with his father's recent death obviously much on his mind, he spoke of "the actor [who] sometimes comes from scenes of affliction and misfortune—even from death itself—to play his part before us."[10] While he was speaking, Dora took a sudden turn for the worse. A family servant was sent to the London tavern. Forster intercepted the messenger and decided to wait until after Dickens had finished his speech to break the news. Together with Mark Lemon, he told Dickens that Dora had died. A month later, on May 18, in a letter to the Count D'Orsay, and with the additional distance afforded by writing in (somewhat fractured) French, Dickens summarized the sad domestic events of March and April as follows:

> La mort de mon pauvre père m'a donné beaucoup de chagrin, et m'a occupé de beaucoup d'affaires. Ma femme ne se

> portait pas bien, et nous allames a Malvern—the cold water cure. En attendant, quand elle commença reprendre ses forces j'allai à Londres, un jour pour presider à "un diner publique." J'avais laissé a Devonshire Terrace, sur l'instant, notre petite Dora. Quand je quittai la table Forster me dit "La petite est morte." (6: 391)

The days and weeks that followed Dora's death were very difficult for the entire family. Dickens wrote to Catherine that night, urging her to return immediately to London and warning her of what she might find there, but without telling her explicitly that Dora was dead. "My dearest Kate," he wrote,

> Now observe. You must read this letter, very slowly and carefully. If you have hurried on thus far without quite understanding (apprehending some bad news), I rely on your turning back, and reading again.
>
> Little Dora, without being in the least pain, is suddenly stricken ill. She awoke out of a sleep, and was seen, in one moment, to be very ill. Mind! I will not deceive you. I think her very ill.
>
> There is nothing in her appearance but perfect rest. You would suppose her quietly asleep. But I am sure she is very ill, and I cannot encourage myself with much hope of her recovery. I do not—why should I say I do, to you my dear!—I do not think her recovery at all likely. (6: 353)

Dickens sat up through the night with his daughter's body, accompanied by his friend Mark Lemon, to whom he wrote several years later in thanks. "I have not forgotten (and never shall forget) who sat up with me one night when a little place in my house was left empty" (7: 599; April 26, 1855).

According to his daughter Mamie, Dickens bore up well at first. He did not break down, she wrote in her memoir, until "an evening or two after her death, [when] some beautiful flowers were sent"; he "was about to take them upstairs and place them on the little dead baby, when he suddenly gave way completely."[11] The only report we have of

Catherine's response to the news of her daughter's death comes in a letter dated April 17 from Forster to Dr. Wilson. "We had a sorrowful journey enough," he tells Wilson, speaking of his trip with Catherine from Malvern back to London, "but I really think that Mrs. Dickens is somewhat better since her return. She grieves bitterly, of course—but I fancy the grief & suffering less morbid than it was for the first twelve hours" (6: 353, n4). On the same day, in a letter to F. M. Evans, Dickens wrote, "Mrs. Dickens is as well as I could hope. I am not without some impression that this shock may even do her good" (6: 355).

The funeral took place on April 17. "We laid the child in her grave today," he wrote to Miss Coutts (6: 356). Exactly where the body was placed is unclear. We know that it was at Highgate cemetery in a pre-existing vault or catacomb, for Dickens subsequently made arrangements for the infant's coffin to be moved to a permanent gravesite with a marble tablet. In early March 1852, nearly a year after Dora's death and soon after the first number of *Bleak House* appeared, he wrote to Forster: "My Highgate journey yesterday was a sad one. . . . I went up to the cemetery to look for a piece of ground . . . in a foolish dislike to leaving the little child shut up in a vault there" (6: 622–23). In May of 1854, nine months after the final number of *Bleak House* had appeared, he wrote to Miss Coutts and mentions having seen "Holly Lodge [the estate in Highgate where Miss Coutts lived], from the outside, looking beautiful." He then adds parenthetically, "(I have just been arranging a very small freehold not far from it, where my little child Dora, of the ill-omened name, is to lie under the sun instead of remaining in a Vault; and whither my many walks in that neighborhood will take me, I suppose, at last)" (7: 337; May 23, 1854). Thoughts of Dora, his many visits to Highgate, and intimations of his own mortality mingle in this sentence, enclosed in a parenthesis and joined by the verb with which Esther Woodcourt would "close" her narrative: "I suppose."

The conception and composition of *Bleak House,* especially in its early stages, were accompanied by unusual signs of restlessness on Dickens's part. The first idea for the novel, as already mentioned, came to him from the "shadows" in February 1851. As the time to begin actually writing approached, Dickens grew increasingly uneasy. On August 17, 1851, he wrote to Miss Coutts from Broadstairs: "I begin to be pondering afar off, a new book. Violent restlessness, and vague ideas of going I don't know where, I don't know why, are the present symptoms of the disorder" (6: 463). Could Dickens possibly not have known that it was the day after what would have been Dora's first birthday? Did he remember that August 17 was the one-year anniversary of his writing, also from Broadstairs, to tell Catherine of her baby's "failure," or that a few days later he had written in separate letters to inform Catherine and Forster that he was "killing" Dora Copperfield?

Forster reports observing similar symptoms during his early August fortnight visit to Broadstairs. "I had not left him many days," Forster writes, "when these lines followed me":

> "I very nearly packed up a portmanteau and went away, the day before yesterday, into the mountains of Switzerland, alone! Still the victim of an intolerable restlessness, I shouldn't be at all surprised if I wrote to you one of these mornings from under Mont Blanc. I sit down between whiles to think of a new story, and, as it begins to grow, such a torment of desire to be anywhere but where I am; and to be going I don't know where, I don't know why; takes hold of me, that it is like being *driven away*."[12]

The "torment of desire" described here is a version of the familiar Dickensian "attraction of repulsion"—a desire to begin writing the story and at the same time to escape from writing it, a simultaneous wish to know and not to know. Like Esther, Dickens had "a great deal of difficulty in beginning to write [his] portion of these pages."

In the letter to Forster mentioned above, written in early March 1852, only days after the first monthly number of *Bleak House* had appeared and as he struggled to complete monthly number 3, containing the scene in which Esther reports witnessing the death of the brickmaker's baby, Dickens writes: "Wild ideas are upon me of going to Paris—Rouen—Switzerland—somewhere—and writing the remaining two-thirds of the next No. aloft in some queer inn room. I have been hanging over it, and have got restless" (6: 623). The letter begins with the mention that Dickens's visit to Highgate "yesterday" was a sad one.

There are many parallels and points of intersection between *Bleak House* and the story (or stories) I have just extracted from Dickens's letters and the other sources that deal with the period between August 1850 and the publication of the final monthly number of *Bleak House* in September 1853. Undeniably, the short life and sudden death of Dora Annie Dickens were much on her father's mind during the time when he contemplated and wrote the novel. We should resist the temptation, however, to force these parallels too closely or try to shine too bright a light on the shadowy zone that lies between the story of Dickens, Catherine, and Dora on the one hand, and that of Esther Woodcourt, Lady Dedlock, Captain Hawdon, and Esther Summerson on the other. No simple equation or one-to-one correspondence exists between the two stories. Moreover, many documents are missing. There are no letters from Catherine during this time and of course nothing from Dora. Likewise, although they are finally recovered by Bucket and returned presumably to Sir Leicester, the letters between Honoria Barbary and Captain Hawdon are never revealed. For all these reasons, it is important to proceed with caution in offering tentative interpretations.

Both Newsom and subsequently Welsh have stressed the importance of John Dickens's death as part of the context in which *Bleak House* was written, but neither critic, I believe, has taken this observation far enough. Dickens had already painted a rich and unforgettable portrait of his father in the figure of Micawber in *David Copperfield*. Perhaps for this reason, he did not feel the need to memorialize his father again in such full detail in his next novel. Nevertheless, John Dickens is present in *Bleak House*. I have already suggested that Harold Skimpole may reflect Dickens's own wish-fulfilling fantasy of a life without responsibilities and that Skimpole's memoir may be a self-conscious parody of the autobiographical fragment, but is Skimpole not also a remembrance, in a different key, of both Micawber and John Dickens? Like Micawber (and Dickens's father), Skimpole has a distinctive rhetoric and a childish relation to money. Like both, he is forever in debt and always at risk of being seized by the bailiff's men. Like both, he is principally indebted to a character who in several ways resembles John Dickens's son: David in the earlier book, Jarndyce in *Bleak House*. Skimpole's memoir, with its accusation of selfishness against Jarndyce, may even suggest a recognition on Dickens's part that his father resented being so dependent on his son and believed that this son was never as generous as he should have been.

The possibility that in Skimpole Dickens was revisiting the figure of Micawber suggests another dimension of self-referentiality in *Bleak House*: the idea of intra-Dickensian intertextuality—of Chadband as a reprise of Stiggins, of Tulkinghorn as a reprise of Carker, of the Bagnets as a reprise of the Peggottys, and so on. Stanley Friedman has written persuasively on the parallels between *Oliver Twist* and *Bleak House*, emphasizing similarities of plot as well as characterization.[13] One of the major literary influences on Dickens was always Dickens himself.

Skimpole is not the only figure in *Bleak House* in whom traces of John Dickens can be found. Another debtor in the book, Gridley, the man from Shropshire, struggles (like Micawber) to free himself from entanglements with the law by writing endless unsuccessful petitions; unlike Micawber, however, he dies. Gridley's is not the first death in the novel, but his is the first deathbed scene. Many of the book's "good" characters gather at his bedside in George's Shooting Gallery: George, Phil Squod, Esther, Miss Flite, Jarndyce, Richard (who will soon take Gridley's place as Chancery suitor), and even Bucket, disguised here as a doctor. We even learn that Bucket has been spying on Gridley from the skylight in the Shooting Gallery. Bucket here may be a stand-in for Dickens, who sat with his father during his final hours, and the group of characters who gather at Gridley's bedside recalls the family and friends who were with John Dickens at the end. If Skimpole is a brief comic encore performance for his father, in Gridley Dickens gave him a sentimental farewell.

The Dora material is much more complicated, and it is difficult to know where to begin. The first question, impossible to answer, is why Dickens chose to give his daughter the "ill-omened name" to begin with. What could he possibly have been thinking? Everything begins with that name. One complication here, of course, is that Dora was originally a fictional character before she was a child. Moreover, as a character in *Copperfield*, she is both a child (a "child-wife," the term she asks David to use for her) and a mother—the mother of a dead child (her miscarriage or stillbirth in chapter 48). Dora doesn't just die in *Copperfield*;

Dickens "kills" her, as he jokingly insists to Catherine and Forster on repeated occasions. Moreover, he "kills" her in the days shortly after his own Dora was born. Just as Esther fantasizes about herself, Dora is born and then dies within a few hours or days thereafter. Alive in London, Dora is considered a "failure" in Broadstairs. Learning that she is tiny and incapable of speech (remember Caddy's deaf and dumb baby), Dickens's son Sydney "gave her up after that." Or so Dickens, in his role as epistolary narrator, reports. Did Dickens also "give her up"?

Alive and at the same time dead, Dora already resembles Esther, a living ghost. Likewise, Dora's mother is both dead and alive. In *Copperfield*, Dora's father, Mr. Spenlow, is a widower; Dora has no mother. Similarly, Catherine Dickens is "dead"—dead in the sense that André Green intends in his essay "The Dead Mother"; that is, she is alive but melancholy and emotionally unavailable to her baby. Resemblances thus begin to thicken between Catherine and Lady Dedlock. Both suffer from nervous depression; both have "dead" babies; and both are cold: Lady Dedlock in her "freezing mood" and later in her exhausted walking from Saint Albans to London in the snow; Catherine in her cold-water cure at Malvern. "It was my mother cold and dead."

As a result of Catherine's nervous depression, the baby is separated from its mother—"abandoned," if you will, and left in the care of unknown servants, the mother's sister (here Georgina), and the baby's father, who also regularly "abandons" it in order to attend to his many worldly obligations, just as he had "abandoned" it on the day it was born in order to go to Broadstairs and finish "killing" Dora. The father (like Hawdon) is thus also absent or "dead," but (in Dickens's case) still alive. The father (Dickens) sometimes plays the role of mother, has the baby brought to his office, plays with it, was "nursing" it on the night he left to go to the Theatrical Fund dinner. Thus, the father (as mother) "abandons" Dora on the night she dies.

Forster is the one who tells Dickens that Dora has died. "La petite est morte" is the way Dickens represents Forster's words, transposing them into French. "The child died" is how Esther reports the death of Jenny's baby. *Bleak House* abounds in dead and dying infants: Caddy's ink-stained baby; Sir Leicester felled by a stroke ("Regard him! The poor infant!" cries Hortense just before Bucket leads her away [837]); Nemo, lying dead in the ink-stained room "with no more track behind him, that any one can trace, than a deserted infant" (173).[14]

The mother of the dead child. The mother of the dead child. The phrase that Esther keeps repeating to herself (and that continues to haunt my own experience of reading this novel) is also the phrase in which Dickens comes closest to actually naming his wife Catherine's—and his own—experience of losing their infant daughter. Who then is "the mother of the dead child"? Catherine certainly, but also Dickens? Georgina? Lady Dedlock? Miss Barbary? Mrs. Rachael? Jenny? Caddy? Dora Copperfield? Until her son George shows up unexpectedly late in the novel as if returning miraculously from the dead, even Mrs. Rouncewell could be numbered among the women in the book who have lost a child. Practically every mother in *Bleak House*, with the exception of Mrs. Bagnet, is a candidate for the role. And which dead child? Dora and Esther, to begin with, but all the others too, including the "something wet" that Bucket and the policeman turn over down by the river at the beginning of the search for Lady Dedlock.

Lady Dedlock is the dead mother, a version of Catherine. But Catherine is also Esther. Her "giddiness and dimness of sight," as Dickens described them to Dr. Wilson, are like the symptoms of Esther's illness. Esther's blank depression and even her near-psychotic visions as she approaches the graveyard ("great water-gates . . . opening and closing in my head") may owe something to Catherine's "morbid" condition, as Forster described it, or to the "alarming disposition of blood to the head" that Dickens mentioned to Wilson and described as "not at all a new disorder with her." Likewise, Dickens's letter to Catherine preparing her for the news of Dora's death—"Now observe. You must read this letter, very slowly and carefully. If you have hurried on thus far without quite understanding (apprehending some bad news), I rely on your turning back, and reading again"—sounds like Bucket trying to warn Esther about what she will find when she reaches the body lying at the graveyard gate: "Miss Summerson, you'll understand me, if you think a moment. They changed clothes at the cottage" (915). In both, the husband/detective/psychoanalyst tries to ease the blow of painful truth for the wife/client/patient whose dissociated condition prevents her from realizing what she already "knows" unconsciously.

Esther is the hardest to talk about. She is a refraction of Dora Annie, of course. She is also Dickens's fantasy of what might have happened if Dora had not died on April 15, but had survived, been raised by someone else, grown to be a young woman, a living ghost, and had reappeared in Catherine and Dickens's life. Would her parents have recognized her? Would they have embraced her? Would they have been "faithful"? Or would they have abandoned her again, found her a "failure," subjected her to another "betrayal"? Would Dickens, in his role as father, novelist, mesmerist, and detective, have been able to restore her to life? Or would she, like Eurydice, have sunk again into the shadowy world? And which would be better, a happy half-life as some version of Dame Durden, the doctor's wife, or the life of a ghostwriter, the life of a ghost?

Dickens grew increasingly restless as he came closer to beginning *Bleak House*. He threw himself into other activities, notably moving from Devonshire Terrace to Tavistock House and taking charge of managing all the decorations and alterations in his new home, so that he could postpone beginning to write for another couple of months. He "knew" at some level—how consciously is impossible to say—that the story of Dora was at the heart of the novel he would write, and he kept returning to Highgate, to her grave, since that was his source of inspiration, the shadowy world from which his story would emerge. At the same time, he wanted to be anywhere else but at the beginning of that story—in Paris, Rouen, or Switzerland. He wanted to begin writing, but felt "*driven away*." To write the story of Dora, of Esther, would require him to face his own responsibility for having "killed" Dora and, in a sense, for having "killed" her mother as well, or at least having helped drive her into depression. No wonder he wanted desperately to be somewhere else. Removing her body from the "vault" and placing it "under the sun" was one small way of making amends (hence Esther Summer-sun?). But nothing could bring Dora Annie back, and Dickens of course knew this. All he could do, the best he could do, was to stop postponing the novel and begin to write it.

To do so meant to open the doors of his bleak house and his unconscious mind to ghosts of the dead. It meant writing about ghosts, not just from the detached perspective of an outside narrator safely removed from the shadowy world, in other words, from the perspective of the unnamed present-tense narrator. It also meant writing from the viewpoint and in the voice of a ghost. Two narrators were needed and two focalizers for the illustrations, one outside the ghost story and the other inside.[15] In order to go inside, Dickens had to switch genders and become Dora; he had to let himself die and at the same time remain alive, and then try to imagine what the condition of living death was like. The strangeness of Esther Woodcourt's voice is one result of this effort.

At the same time that he was trying to write the story of Dora, or a version of it, Dickens was also writing his own story. "I hope any one who may read what I write, will understand that if these pages contain a great deal about me, I can only suppose it must be because I have really something to do with them, and can't be kept out." *Bleak House* is a giant assembly room of Dickensian mirrors. Esther's descent into the world of her unconscious is also Dickens's descent into a personal past—into memories of the blacking factory, his dead father, his dead child, and perhaps also, at a great remove, into memories of his own infancy and of a mother who disappointed him, as all mothers do. It is also a descent into the haunted house of English history.

6

SPECTERS

LARGELY MISSING FROM THE READING THAT I HAVE BEEN DEveloping thus far has been much acknowledgment of the fact that *Bleak House* is a major social novel, a "condition of England" novel written soon after the end of one of the most tumultuous and embattled decades of the century, the 1840s, and it is to this aspect of the book that I now want to turn. Critical discussions of the novel from this perspective have taken a number of different approaches, focusing, for example, on *Bleak House* as Dickens's response to the Great Exhibition of 1851 and as his dark commentary on the celebration of British industrial and commercial power manifested in the construction and contents of the Crystal Palace.[1] Other discussions have focused on the novel's discourses of empire and race, its critique of Chancery, its analysis of dandyism in religion, its condemnation of misguided or "telescopic" philanthropy, and its references to science.[2] In an important and highly influential essay, D. A. Miller has developed a powerful Foucauldian reading of the novel, arguing that the Bagnet family's catchphrase, "Discipline must be maintained," identifies a central thematic and structural feature of the novel: its exercise of external and internal surveillance over characters in the book and its controlling effect on the reader, who must submit to the regular discipline of industrial society by purchasing and consuming serial installments over the course of the novel's nineteen-month schedule of publication.³

Other influential readings of the book's social themes have centered on questions of gender and class. Critics worry about the extent to which *Bleak House* is complicit with dominant attitudes toward the position of women in nineteenth-century society or, on the contrary, challenges Victorian gender stereotypes. Similarly, they argue about where the novel stands on issues of class. Clearly Dickens condemns the neglect of poor and outcast members of society, but does he also endorse the Ironmaster? And does the novel's reliance on the marriage plot to provide formal and ideological closure indicate its acquiescence to a middle-class worldview and its retreat from intractable social problems in favor of easier domestic solutions? Hilary Schor's discussion of *Bleak House* in terms of women's legal position in society is an example of the insights that the best feminist scholarship can bring to the novel.⁴ Chris R. Vanden Bossche's study of the multiple and sometimes conflicting class discourses that the novel presents is an equally fine discussion of this aspect of the book.⁵

My own view of the novel's social and political concerns adopts a somewhat more historical approach and takes as its point of departure a simple question: if *Bleak House* is a ghost story, who are its ghosts?⁶ In a sense, this is a question that I have been answering from the outset. *Bleak House* has many ghosts, and I have already mentioned a goodly number of them. Ghosts appear in practically every chapter of the book. There are comic ghosts, beginning with Snagsby's deceased partner in the firm of Peffer and Snagsby and extending to the members of the *danse macabre* in chapter 66, led by the "tuckered sylph" Volumnia. Another comic ghost is the suspicious Mrs. Snagsby, skulking around at night to discover evidence of her husband's infidelity and turning their Cursitor Street residence into a haunted house. "Mrs. Snagsby is so perpetually on the alert, that the house becomes ghostly with creaking boards and rustling garments. The 'prentices think somebody may have been murdered there, in bygone times" (408).

The list of figurative ghosts in the novel is quite various. Before Krook goes up in smoke, Guppy's friend Tony Jobling (aka Weevle), refers to him as "old Boguey downstairs" (509), and after he has disappeared,

Krook's room is described as "ghostly with traces of its dead inhabitant, and even with his chalked writing on the wall" (634). When the Court goes on its long vacation, the "good ships Law and Equity" are compared to "the Flying Dutchman, with a crew of ghostly clients imploring all whom they may encounter to peruse their papers" (300). At one point Judy Smallweed gives her grandfather a "ghostly poke" (428) in the ribs. After the election in which Sir Leicester's party is defeated and when Tulkinghorn announces his intention to tell a story, which turns out to be the allegorical story of Lady Dedlock's sexual indiscretion, Volumnia is "enchanted. A story! O he is going to tell something at last! A ghost in it, Volumnia hopes?" (649).

When Bucket first shows up abruptly in Tulkinghorn's room, the narrator comments that there is "nothing remarkable about him at first sight but his ghostly manner of appearing" (355). When Esther recalls seeing Ada at the piano in Jarndyce's Bleak House with Richard standing next to her, she writes, "Upon the wall, their shadows blended together, surrounded by strange forms, not without a ghostly motion caught from the unsteady fire, though reflected from motionless objects" (93). At one point Guster, the Snagsbys' servant, "comes rustling and scratching down the little staircase like a popular ghost" (304). When the servant leaves him in the dimly lit library of the house in town where he has his first interview with Lady Dedlock, "Mr. Guppy looks into the shade in all directions, discovering everywhere a certain charred and whitened little heap of coal or wood. Presently he hears a rustling. Is it—? No, it's no ghost; but fair flesh and blood, most brilliantly dressed" (533). The ghost of Krook is on his mind, but it is Lady Dedlock who appears out of the shadows.

Even Allan Woodcourt, perhaps the least likely figure in the book to wear such an attribution, is compared to an apparition.

> "Woodcourt, my dear fellow!" cried Richard, starting up with extended hands, "you come upon my vision like a ghost."
>
> "A friendly one," he replied, "and only waiting, as they say ghosts do, to be addressed. How does the mortal world go?" (781)

Another unlikely ghost is little Peepy Jellyby, the child whom Esther rescued soon after her arrival in London. At the end of chapter 4, Esther reports drifting off to sleep and losing hold of her own identity, which mingles with that of Caddy, Ada, her friends at Reading, and Miss Flite. "I began to lose the identity of the sleeper resting on me," she writes. "Now, it was Ada; now, one of my old Reading friends. . . . Now, it was the little mad woman worn out with curtseying and smiling. . . . Lastly, it was no one, and I was no one." When she wakes the next morning, Esther writes, "I opened my eyes to encounter those of a dirty-faced little spectre fixed upon me. Peepy had scaled his crib, and crept down in his bedgown and cap, and was so cold that his teeth were chattering as if he had cut them all" (63).

FIG. 10. "Sunset in the long Drawing-room at Chesney Wold."

Haunted houses abound in the novel, chief among them Chesney Wold, with its Ghost's Walk terrace and its ever-deepening shadows. As the golden sunset bathes the windows of the house in a rich glow, shadows encroach on the drawing room, and the house comes strangely alive: "Then do the frozen Dedlocks thaw. Strange movements come upon their features, as the shadows of leaves play there. A dense Justice in a corner is beguiled into a wink. A staring Baronet, with a truncheon, gets a dimple on his chin. . . . A maid of honour of the court of Charles the Second, with large round eyes (and other charms to correspond), seems to bathe in glowing water, and it ripples as it glows" (641). The accompanying illustration, "Sunset in the long Drawing-room at Chesney Wold" (fig. 10), can thus be understood as depicting a gallery of ghosts.

Since no living human figure is mentioned as present on the scene, the focalization of this image, if internal, must be from the homoperceptive viewpoint of a fellow ghost; if external, from the heteroperceptive viewpoint of the "narrator"; or else, in free indirect perception, from both.

The novel's two principal ghosts, as I have argued at length, are Lady Dedlock and Esther, both "dead" in different ways, but both manifestly alive. Both dwell in the shadows and try to hide themselves from view. Both move about at dusk or in the night. Both walk along the Ghost's Walk terrace. Each returns from being "dead" to haunt the other. When Lady Dedlock leaves the house in town for good, her departure is ghostly; she "leaves all her jewels and her money, listens, goes downstairs at a moment when the hall is empty, opens and shuts the great door; flutters away, in the shrill frosty wind" (856). Both Esther and Lady Dedlock "die" a second time in the course of the narrative—Esther from disease, her mother from "exposure"—but both have trouble staying dead. Both, in the interpretation I have offered of the novel's final illustration, still linger in the vicinity of the Dedlock family mausoleum. Esther's spectral emanation takes yet another form—the uncanny narrative voice that I have called her "ghostwriting."

The novel's long list of literal and figurative apparitions is shadowed by the ghosts that emerge from Dickens's past. These include fictional as well as biographical ghosts. The list might begin with Dora Spenlow Copperfield ("killed" by Dickens on or about August 20, 1850) as well as her dead baby. We could go back even farther and recall that David is a "posthumous child" whose father dies before he is born. In chapter 1 of *Copperfield,* David confidently reports that, despite predictions at the time of his birth that he would be "privileged to see ghosts and spirits," he has not come into "that part of my inheritance."[7] Despite his statement to the contrary, ghosts—especially paternal ghosts—soon begin to appear in David's narrative: Dr. Chillip, who "walked as softly as the Ghost in Hamlet";[8] the pasty-faced and violently named Mr. Murdstone, who resembles a figure from the waxworks; and even the ghost of David's father, metamorphosed into scary long-necked geese, a large dog, and associations with the biblical story of Lazarus. Anticipated in David's rich fantasy life (however much he may deny such visionary powers), the ghost of Dickens's own father, dead on March 31,

1851, hovers over the composition of *Bleak House* and inflects the figures of Skimpole and Gridley.

As the previous chapter has argued, the principal biographical ghost threading its way though the pages of *Bleak House* is that of Dora Annie Dickens, dead on April 15, 1851. Images of dead and dying infants are everywhere in the novel. The ghost of Dora appears most vividly, however, in the person of Esther Summerson, walking along the terrace at Chesney Wold, and in the ghostly retrospective voice of Esther Woodcourt. As Dickens moved closer to beginning the novel, thoughts of Dora were often on his mind and in his letters. He could not stay away from her, although he seems to have tried, throwing himself into other tasks. He visited her gravesite, even imagined himself joining her eventually in Highgate cemetery. As the novel approached its conclusion, he could not let her body lie still, insisting finally that it be moved from the vault where it had first been laid to a sunny "freehold." Even his public speaking engagements during this time betray a more personal interest. He espoused the cause of public sanitation in the wake of Edwin Chadwick's famous 1842 report and focused attention particularly on graveyard reform. The pestilential graveyard where Nemo is buried would of course be a central location in *Bleak House*.[9] Much as he felt "*driven away*" from beginning to write the novel, as he wrote to Forster in August, he found ways of returning to the shadowy world where Dora lay. She was his inspiration, the ghost as muse.

The list of *Bleak House* ghosts is by no means exhausted. I have barely mentioned the novel's earliest ghost, that of the first Lady Dedlock, whose story Mrs. Rouncewell tells in chapter 7. This is the novel's original specter, its ur-ghost, so to speak. The location of this chapter is also significant. At the end of chapter 6, Esther writes that she pulled herself away from speculating about who her father might be, addressed herself in the third person with a call to "Duty," shook her housekeeping keys, and "rang me hopefully to bed" (103). At the beginning of chapter 8, Esther resumes her story, presumably at the point where she left off at the end of chapter 6. She describes dressing herself in the morning and staring out the window where her two candles, "reflected in the black panes like two beacons" (114), stare back at her like eyes. Chapter 7, the intervening chapter, in which the ghost story is told, is thus situated during a time when Esther is asleep. The unnamed present-tense narrator even goes out of his (or is it her?) way to emphasize the temporal continuity here, beginning chapter 7 with an unusual transition: "While Esther sleeps, and while Esther wakes, it is still wet weather down at the place in Lincolnshire" (103). Is this Esther third-personing herself again, this time in the voice of the other narrator? In any event, chapter 7 is situated during the night while Esther sleeps and thus might be understood, in some shadowy way, as Esther's dream, a product or reflection of her unconscious mind—or of an unconscious that she shares with other English men and women.[10]

The story that Mrs. Rouncewell tells is crucial to an understanding of *Bleak House*. Foundational in the history of the Dedlock family, it is also foundational in the history of England. The story recounts an episode in the great national narrative of the English Civil War. According to Mrs. Rouncewell, the story of the first Lady Dedlock took place "In the wicked days, my dears, of King Charles the First." She then hastens to correct herself, adding "I mean, of course, in the wicked days of the rebels who leagued themselves against that excellent King" (112). Her slip of the tongue is "of course" significant and reveals her bias as well as the potential for bias in any historical narrative. The judgment of who was "wicked" and who was not will depend on the perspective of the storyteller. Mrs. Rouncewell is not an unprejudiced narrator. Nevertheless, her story contains elements that can be read against the grain of her intentions.

Sir Morbury Dedlock, Lady Dedlock's husband, she continues, "was . . . on the side of the blessed martyr. But it *is* supposed that his lady, who had none of the family blood in her veins, favoured the bad cause" (112). She had "relations" among the king's enemies, "was in correspondence with them," and gave them information, spying on the country gentlemen who met at Chesney Wold from outside the door of their council room. Relations between Lady Dedlock and her husband worsened. In addition to their political differences, they "were not well suited to each other in age or character, and they had no children to moderate between them. After her favourite brother, a young gentleman, was killed in the civil wars (by Sir Morbury's near kinsman), her feeling was so violent that she hated the race into which she had married" (113). The story concludes with Mrs. Rouncewell's account of how the Ghost's Walk came to have its name. After having been apprehended by her husband in an attempt to lame his favorite horse, as she had lamed others in his stable belonging to supporters of the king, Lady Dedlock fell or was thrown by her husband or kicked by the horse—in any event, she was injured and permanently lamed in the hip. Ever afterward, rejecting any assistance from her husband, the injured woman walked up and down, up and down, along the terrace, refusing to be reconciled and pronouncing a curse upon the "pride" of the Dedlock house, until it has been humbled. "When calamity, or when disgrace is coming to it," she tells her husband, "let the Dedlocks listen for my step!" (113).

It takes little effort to see the parallels between this narrative and the story of the current Lady Dedlock—also married to an older man, with no children to moderate between herself and her husband, having had "relations" with a man of a different class, "in correspondence" with him, closely tied to a "young gentleman" now deceased, herself of a different class background, and so on. The term "favourite brother" in Mrs. Rouncewell's story may even be a euphemism for "lover." The fall and injury to the first Lady Dedlock's body are the physical mark of a rift between husband and wife, but also of the antagonism between their social classes and political parties. The curse of the first Lady Dedlock and the injury to her body are thus the signs of an unhealed wound, a wound dating from two centuries earlier (the 1640s) that still insists on being heard in the Victorian age (the 1840s). It manifests itself as "an echo that is only heard after dark, and is often unheard for a long while together. But it comes back, from time to time.... That is the story. Whatever the sound is," Mrs. Rouncewell concludes, "it is a worrying sound ... and what is to be noticed in it, is, that it *must be heard*" (114; emphasis in the original).

The history of England, this story suggests, is the story of a trauma, inscribed on a woman's body and, although silent for long periods of time, insistently returning in times of crisis. As Caruth points out in *Unclaimed Experience,* trauma is "always the story of a wound that cries out, that addresses us in the attempt to tell us of a reality or truth that is not otherwise available." Just as the plot of Esther Summerson and Lady Dedlock can be understood as a psychological story of trauma and the return of unbidden memories from the past, so the novel's political plot takes the form of a historical ghost story centered on an episode of injury—a story that repeats itself as an echo that *must be heard*.

The story that Mrs. Rouncewell tells to her grandson and Rosa at Chesney Wold is meant to be sympathetic to the king, "the blessed martyr," and his supporters, but it lends itself readily to a different interpretation. From another perspective, we could say that the original Lady Dedlock is the blessed martyr, a martyr in the struggle against class oppression and royal usurpation of power, and that a truth "not otherwise available" has already emerged in Mrs. Rouncewell's verbal slip when she speaks of the "wicked days of King Charles the First." Understood in this way, the original ghost of Chesney Wold is a figure of resistance that continues to haunt the house of England and that returns from time to time whenever the original injuries of the civil war are reactivated in a new historical context by the struggle between established power and the needs of the people. The old ghost story that Mrs. Rouncewell tells is thus a national allegory, whose subtext has fresh relevance for the nineteenth century, although the cast of characters and the issues at stake are no longer quite the same.

It is important to note in passing that chapter 7 of *Bleak House* contains two female figures who by no means conform to the gender stereotypes of the proper Victorian lady. One is Mrs. Rouncewell, the old housekeeper who plays the part of oral historian or national bard and on whose "mind," the narrator tells us, "the whole house reposes" (105). She is the "housekeeper," the storyteller who "keeps" national memory alive and to whom the "house" of the nation may more properly belong than it does to the titular owner of the estate. The second "improper" lady is Lady Dedlock herself—out in the stables at night, laming horses, struggling with a man, refusing assistance, uttering curses. Not exactly an angel in the house. Mrs. Rouncewell is of course from the serving class and Lady Dedlock from another historical era, but their presence in the text suggests that *Bleak House* contains a wider spectrum of female characters than is often supposed.

To read the ghost story of chapter 7 as an allegory of the English national past and the family ghost of Chesney Wold as a specter haunting the house of England is to turn from figurative and biographical ghosts to historical ones. It is also the moment to set *Bleak House* alongside Dickens's often-neglected historical text, *A Child's History of England*, composed and published during the very same years, 1851–53, when he was writing the novel. Precisely because it is a history meant for children and because it was largely dictated (to Georgina, perhaps to other scribes at *Household Words*) rather than entirely written down by Dickens, *A Child's History* has not been taken as seriously as it deserves to be, nor has its relevance for *Bleak House* been fully explored.[11]

An oral history addressed to the young, *A Child's History* resembles in these respects the story that Mrs. Rouncewell tells to Watt and Rosa, but on a much larger scale and with a very different emphasis. Rather than a defense of monarchy and established order, Dickens's history of England is a long catalog of misrule and abusive autocratic power, punctuated by episodes of mostly unsuccessful popular resistance. Philip Collins accurately characterizes the book's view of history as "a projection back over the centuries" of Dickens's "political creed," as stated in Birmingham in 1869: "My faith in the people governing is, on the whole, infinitesimal; my faith in The People governed, is, on the whole, illimitable."[12]

A Child's History consists largely of a chronicle of heroes and villains. Staunchly Protestant and anti-Catholic (the Druid priesthood comes in for a fair amount of criticism early on, anticipating such detested later figures as Archbishop Laud), the book is short on dates and long on battles, the bloodier the better. Dickens apparently believed that descriptions of mortal combat, assassination, torture, and mass slaughter would hold children's attention; successful purveyors of mass media in subsequent centuries have not proved him wrong. Although it ends with a conventional toast to Queen Victoria ("God Save the Queen!"), the book is also to a great extent antimonarchist. Its villains include virtually every English ruler from ancient times to 1688, with special attention to Henry the Eighth ("a disgrace to human nature, and a blot of blood and grease upon the History of England") and Charles the First. The only monarch to receive unequivocal praise is Alfred the Great. Dickens's summary evaluation of Alfred is notable for its relevance to *Bleak House*. (I quote the chapter's final paragraph in full.)

> I pause to think with admiration, of the noble king who, in his single person, possessed all the Saxon virtues. Whom misfortune could not subdue, whom prosperity could not spoil, whose perseverance nothing could shake. Who was hopeful in defeat, and generous in success. Who loved justice, freedom, truth, and knowledge. Who, in his care to instruct his people, probably did more to preserve the beautiful old Saxon language, than I can imagine. Without whom the English tongue in which I tell this story might have wanted half its meaning. As it is said that his spirit still inspires some of our best English laws, so, let you and I pray that it may animate our English hearts, at least to this—to resolve, when we see any of our fellow-creatures left in ignorance, that we will do our best, while life is in us, to have them taught; and to tell those rulers whose duty it is to teach them, and who neglect their duty, that they have profited very little by all the years that have rolled away since the year nine hundred and one, and that they are far behind the bright example of KING ALFRED THE GREAT.[13]

It is not difficult to hear in these words an echo of Dickens's condemnation of Chancery and his critique of the illiteracy to which Jo is condemned. In its praise for his contributions to the English language, moreover, the paragraph also acknowledges Alfred as one of Dickens's literary ancestors.

Dickens's sympathies throughout the book are with the people—Britons, he calls them, "hardy, brave, and strong" (*CHE* 130)—and with their champions, commoners for the most part, who speak up against oppression in the name of justice, freedom, truth, and knowledge and who on occasion lead popular uprisings against the forces of the state. His list of such champions includes one William Fitz-Osbert, "called LONGBEARD," leader of a twelfth-century secret society, comprising fifty thousand men, that took up the cause of the overtaxed populace under Richard the First. Captured and eventually hanged at Smithfield, Fitz-Osbert anticipates other such popular leaders. Here is how Dickens concludes his account of this brief episode: "Death was long a favourite remedy for silencing the people's advocates; but as we go on with this history, I fancy we shall find them difficult to make an end of, for all that" (*CHE* 229).

Another popular champion who earns Dickens's praise is Wat Tyler, the fourteenth-century leader of a "great confused army of poor men" who rose in protest against the poll tax. Tyler of course appears in *Bleak House*, where he looms threateningly in Sir Leicester's imagination as the prototypical leader of popular insurrection (reflecting contemporary upper-class fears of Chartism and similar movements of the 1840s). Betrayed and savagely murdered, Tyler is another martyr to the people's cause. Dickens makes his admiration for Tyler clear: "Wat was a hard-working man, who had suffered much, and had been foully outraged; and it is probable that he was a man of a much higher nature and a much braver spirit than any of the parasites who exulted then, or have exulted since, over his defeat" (*CHE* 297). So much, we can conclude, for Sir Leicester's view of relations between the classes, both in the past and in the nineteenth century.

Surprisingly, two leaders of popular uprisings mentioned in *A Child's History* are women. The first is the mythic British queen Boadicea, who led a revolt against the Romans. Dickens imagines her "in a war-chariot, with her fair hair streaming in the wind, and her injured daughters lying at her feet, [driving] among the troops, and [crying] to them for vengeance on their oppressors, the licentious Romans." Her army vanquished, "the unhappy queen took poison" (*CHE* 135). Even more surprising, the second popular heroine of the book is not English, but a Frenchwoman: Joan of Arc. Dickens devotes an entire section of chapter 22 to the Maid of Orleans, more space than he accords to many English monarchs. No doubt his interest in her was based on the likely appeal of her romantic story to children, but it is also her transformation from peasant girl to champion of the people and woman warrior that captures his attention.

After telling her story, Dickens devotes several paragraphs to Joan's capture, imprisonment, witchcraft trial before the Bishop of Beauvais, and eventual incineration at the stake. He describes her end thus: "This shrieking girl—last seen amidst the smoke and fire, holding a crucifix between her hands; last heard, calling upon Christ—was burnt to ashes. They threw her ashes into the river Seine; but they will rise against her murderers on the last day" (*CHE* 329–30). Joan's story has several uncanny distant echoes in *Bleak House*. Like Krook (the comparison is awful), she goes up in flames and is reduced to ashes.[14] Like Esther, she hears strange voices. Like Hortense, she is violent and French. Like the Lady Dedlock of Mrs. Rouncewell's story, she will return as an avenging ghost.

The climax of *A Child's History* is its account of the reign of Charles the First and of the resistance to his autocratic rule, resulting in the overthrow and beheading of the king and the establishment of Cromwell's Protectorate. Critics have largely been of the opinion that *A Child's History* has no particular narrative shape other than its chronology of successive reigns and that, because Dickens was in a hurry to finish, the history ends with only the most perfunctory summary of events since 1688. The reigns of William and Mary, Anne, the four Georges, and William the Fourth, and the first years of Victoria's rule—over 160 years of English history—are telescoped into barely two pages of comment. On closer examination, however, Dickens's history can be seen to have a more shapely narrative than this account suggests. Though loosely structured and based unquestionably in chronology, *A Child's History* resembles a well-planned fictional narrative in several respects. Perhaps not surprisingly, it resembles a Dickens novel.

Taken as a coherent narrative rather than simply as a loosely connected chronicle, *A Child's History of England* moves inexorably toward the chapters devoted to the English Civil War.[15] These events are the subject of Mrs. Rouncewell's ghost story, and they are at the heart of *Bleak House*'s historical vision. In this connection we should recall that Mr. Dick, the simple-minded sage of *David Copperfield*, finds himself unable to complete his "memorial" because "King Charles's head" keeps getting into the story. King Charles also keeps getting into *Bleak House*. Regicide, Civil War, the long bloody English past—these are all pieces of the story coded into the Ghost's Walk refrain: drip, drip, drip. What drips at Chesney Wold is not just rain but the blood of generations of English men and women. The curse on the Dedlock "house" is national as well as domestic.

During the 1840s, beginning with *Chuzzlewit* and continuing in

Dombey and *Copperfield,* Dickens assumed greater control over the form of his sprawling fictional narratives. One characteristic feature of his novels became a climactic event placed near but not at the very end of the story, usually in monthly number 18 of the typical nineteen-month serialization. The chase sequence in chapters 57 to 59 of *Bleak House* is a good example. Devoting his penultimate installment to a dramatic event allowed him to use the final monthly number to wrap up the plot, explain what happened to some of the main characters, and pull together other loose threads. *A Child's History* has a similar structure. Its climactic event is the Civil War; what follows, especially the Restoration and the reign of Charles the Second, is anticlimax. The final chapters are largely an afterthought, a wrap-up that brings things up to the present time.

Read as the climax of *A Child's History,* the chapters devoted to Charles the First and Cromwell help to explain why Mrs. Rouncewell's ghost story is so important for *Bleak House.* Among other things, they recapitulate the long history of royal abuse and popular resistance that forms the basis of Dickens's historical vision—the "fatal division between the King and the people" (*CHE* 453) that he traces over the course of many centuries. The principal villain here is the king, who repeatedly breaks his word, authorizes or condones acts of savage violence against his subjects, and puts down the people's liberties at every opportunity. Here is one of Dickens's summary statements: "For twelve years King Charles the First reigned in England unlawfully and despotically, seized upon his subjects' goods and money at his pleasure, and punished according to his unbridled will all who ventured to oppose him. It is a fashion for some people to think that this King's career was cut short; but I must say myself that I think it ran a pretty long one" (*CHE* 456–57).

The heroes in Dickens's account of this historical period are men like Sir John Eliot, Leighton, Prynne, and Bastwick, all opponents of the king and all imprisoned or brutally tortured by Archbishop Laud and his allies. The two main champions of the people during this time are John Hampden ("the most popular man in England" [*CHE* 458]) and Cromwell, who emerges in Dickens's narrative as a wise leader in a time of national crisis ("he ruled wisely, and as the times required"

[*CHE* 488]). Although he notes Cromwell's devotion to a "gloomy" religion, Dickens praises his "cheerful" disposition and his encouragement of "men of genius and learning," including Milton. Interestingly, in view of his own recent bereavement, Dickens links Cromwell's declining health and eventual death to the loss of his favorite daughter Elizabeth: "He loved this daughter the best of the family, . . . and could hardly be induced to stir from her sick room until she died. . . . He was ill of the gout and ague; and when the death of his beloved child came upon him in addition, he sank, never to raise his head again" (*CHE* 493). Is Cromwell perhaps another oblique biographical refraction of the author, appearing in a most unlikely place, and Elizabeth Cromwell another distant memory of Dora?

If, according to Dickens's allegorical account of his nation's history, Cromwell's Protectorate represents the historical high point of popular political success in England's past, the Restoration and the return of Charles the Second mark a bathetic return to the bad old days of royal privilege and abuse. The chapters devoted to Charles the Second and James the Second are written in a different tone—much more sarcastic and bitter than anything that precedes them, reflecting perhaps the profound sense of anger and disillusionment that Dickens felt at this betrayal of the people's cause. Read against the structure of a Dickens novel, these chapters correspond to the "unhappy ending" that often shadows the more conventional happier closure that his novels typically provide. That "happy ending" appears here in Dickens's closing compliment to the "very good, and much beloved" Queen Victoria and in the perfunctory praise that he accords to the glorious revolution of 1688, very different in its emphasis from Macaulay's well-known celebration of this event.[16] Like a good Dickens novel, *A Child's History* even ends with a marriage: "She was married to PRINCE ALBERT of Saxe-Gotha on the tenth of February, one thousand eight hundred and forty" (*CHE* 531). Marriage here is only a formal device, however, a convenient way to close. As in *Bleak House,* the real endings lie elsewhere.

Read in the way I have suggested, *A Child's History of England* is a "people's history," an allegory more than a work of realism—or rather, like most Dickens novels, a mixture of the two. As allegory, it recounts a history of trauma and repetition, the repetition over many centuries of injuries committed against the people's liberties and their bodies and of heroic but failed attempts to speak out against such abuse. *A Child's History* is also a ghost story. Its ghosts include admirable heroes—Boadicea, Alfred, Wat Tyler, Joan of Arc, Hampden, Cromwell—but also sinister figures—Druids, Romans, Henry the Eighth, the Stuarts, Buckingham, Laud. The story ends effectively in 1688. For a continuation of the story, one must turn to *Bleak House*.

Bleak House is a historical novel, a "historiography of the present," as John Lucas rightly calls it.[17] Like *A Child's History*, it is also a ghost story, and I must now return to a more complete enumeration of the historical ghosts that it contains. In so doing, I want to enlarge the theoretical framework of my discussion and appeal to a more recent analyst of ghosts and ghost stories, Jacques Derrida. Derrida's *Specters of Marx* is a long meditation on the relevance of Marx and Marxism for the current post-Soviet historical moment. It takes its title and point of departure from the opening sentence of the *Communist Manifesto:* "A specter is haunting Europe—the specter of communism." Derrida's analysis—a "hauntology," he punningly calls it—ranges widely, but several aspects of his discussion have particular relevance for *Bleak House*.[18]

First and foremost, we should note the uncanny coincidence of dates. The *Manifesto* dates from 1848, a scant few years before the "first shadows of a new story" began "hovering in a ghostly way about me," as Dickens wrote in a letter of February 1851. Like Marx and Engels, Dickens recognized the presence of a ghost rising at the end of the revolutionary decade. In the "Exordium" attached by way of preface to the printed version of his 1993 lecture series on Marx, Derrida makes a point that resonates strongly with the concerns of Dickens's novel. "If I am getting ready to speak at length," he writes,

> about ghosts, inheritance, and generations, generations of ghosts, which is to say about certain *others* who are not present, nor presently living, either to us, in us, or outside us, it is in the name of *justice*. . . . It is necessary to speak *of the* ghost, indeed *to the* ghost and *with* it, from the moment that no ethics, no politics, whether revolutionary or not, seems possible and thinkable and *just* that does not recognize in its principle

the respect for those others who are no longer or for those others who are not yet *there,* presently living, whether they are already dead or not yet born.¹⁹

Derrida's emphasis on the importance of justice, rather than merely law, is central to *Bleak House*.

A second concern that Derrida shares with Dickens is his insistence on the strange temporality of ghosts. For Derrida, ghosts are not just emanations from the past. They are also very much of the present moment and of a time yet to come. One has but to think of the ghosts in *A Christmas Carol* to recognize Dickens's concurrence on this point. Derrida speaks of "a spectral moment, a moment that no longer belongs to time" (xix). "Haunting," he says, "is historical, to be sure, but it is not *dated*" (3; emphasis in the original). The specter, he continues, remains invisible between its apparitions. It "looks at us and sees us not see it even when it is there. A spectral asymmetry interrupts here all specularity. It de-synchronizes, it recalls us to anachrony" (6). Since we cannot see or identify the ghost with certainty, "we must fall back on its voice" (7). The ghost, he asserts, is inevitably a figure associated with mourning. Citing the opening scenes of *Hamlet,* Derrida probes the meaning of Hamlet's statement: "The time is out of joint." The ghost, Derrida insists, summons Hamlet to "redress history, the *wrong* [tort] of history" (24). In response, Hamlet curses the destiny that has made him

> a righter of wrongs, the one who, like the right, can only come after the crime, or simply *after:* that is, in a necessarily second generation, originarily late and therefore destined to *inherit.* One never inherits without coming to terms with [*s'expliquer avec*] some specter, and therefore with more than one specter. With the fault but also the injunction of *more than one.* That is the originary wrong, the birth wound from which he suffers, a bottomless wound, an irreparable tragedy, the indefinite malediction that marks the history of the law or history as law: that time is "out of joint" is what is also attested by birth itself when it dooms someone to be the man of right and law only by becoming an inheritor, redresser of wrongs. (24–25; emphasis in the original)

Here and throughout the essay, Derrida puns on the words for "right" (*droit,* which also means "law") and "wrong" (*tort,* which also means a legal tort).

Returning to the specter's demand for justice, Derrida invokes the concept of the gift. "The question of justice, the one that always carries beyond the law, is no longer separated . . . from that of the gift. Heidegger interrogates the paradox of this gift without debt and without guilt" (30–31). Derrida goes on to link the notion of the gift to what he calls "the messianic: the coming of the other, the absolute and unpredictable singularity of the *arrivant as justice*" (33; emphasis in the original). There is something utopian for Derrida in this messianic idea of a justice that exceeds "juridical-moral rules, norms, or representations" (34) and that holds out an "emancipatory promise; it is perhaps even the formality of a structural messianism, a messianism without religion, even a messianic without messianism, an idea of justice—which we distinguish from law or right and even from human rights—and an idea of democracy—which we distinguish from its current concept and from its determined predicates today" (74). The specter that comes back from the dead (the *revenant,* in French) may incite fear (the specter of communism as perceived by those who see it as a threat), but it can also elicit the promise of "imminence and desire of resurrection. Re-naissance or *revenance?*" (44; emphasis in the original).

These heady thoughts can bring us back to *Bleak House,* whose ghosts partake of many of the qualities suggested by Derrida's "hauntology." Consider Wat Tyler again, for example. Wat is a ghost from the past, from the Peasants' Revolt of 1381; he is also a ghost of the present moment (Chartist groups adopted his name for their organizations, and one Chartist leader took Wat Tyler as his pseudonym).[20] In his demand for justice on behalf of ordinary people, both then and now, he is also a ghost from and for the future, a figure of "emancipatory promise" in Derrida's terms. For Sir Leicester, Wat Tyler is a specter to be feared; for Dickens, from the perspective of *A Child's History,* Wat is a specter to be welcomed and embraced.

Wat's name has another, more ambiguous echo in the book—Watt Rouncewell, the Ironmaster's son. He too is one of the novel's ghosts, a ghost of the future. In addition to its echo of the thirteenth-century

Wat, Watt's name also recalls James Watt, inventor of the steam engine, and as such it points toward a future marked by the shift from an agriculturally based economy to an industrial one. Watt is generally a positive figure in *Bleak House,* and his marriage to Rosa seems to be a hopeful sign on the whole. How the novel views the shift in political power from Sir Leicester to Watt's father, the Ironmaster, is less clear and is a subject I will take up shortly.

Hortense is another of the novel's ghosts, one that occupies a more troubling place in its array of specters. The embodiment of pure anger and class resentment, she is more to be feared than perhaps any other figure in the book. As many critics have pointed out, she carries associations to the worst excesses of the Terror, specifically to Carlyle's description of "The Insurrection of Women" in book 7 of *The French Revolution.* Esther confirms this connection, likening her to "some woman from the streets of Paris in the reign of terror" (368). A Frenchwoman and a murderess, she would already seem to have two if not three black marks against her, but lest we dismiss her too readily as a case of Dickensian xenophobia and fear of mob violence, we should recall that she also combines aspects of Boadicea and Joan of Arc, two positive heroines from *A Child's History,* and that she carries out what amounts to a political assassination against the most detested figure in the book, performing an act that both Lady Dedlock and Esther have imagined committing and thereby relieving them of the responsibility and the punishment. Hers is also one of the novel's voices calling for justice, albeit more shrilly than the others. In her demands for employment and fair treatment by Lady Dedlock and Tulkinghorn, she speaks on behalf of the servant class, such figures as Guster and Charley Neckett, whose interests had recently been the subject of debate in Parliament and whose protection was a principal goal of the Apprentices and Servants Act of 1851. Still, the novel rests easier when this angry ghost has been spirited offstage in the protective custody of Inspector Bucket.

Two other historical "ghosts" in the novel are invoked by the title of chapter 63: "Steel and Iron." "Steel" is the name by which Mr. George introduces himself to his brother the Ironmaster. "Iron" is of course a reference to Mr. Rouncewell, the factory owner whose political party defeats Sir Leicester's in the national election described in chapter 40. "Steel" is also a reference to George's profession. He is a soldier, and steel is the material from which swords are made. George is mostly a ghost from the past, however—"hardy, brave, and strong" like the Britons whom Dickens praises at the beginning of *A Child's History*. He comes from yeoman stock and is a pillar of honest, simple truth, but he does not fit easily into the modern, urban world of London with its cash economy. It is fitting that he ends up as Sir Leicester's faithful squire, living in the Keeper's lodge at Chesney Wold. The two of them represent the best of what survives from England's feudal past, but they belong to a bygone era. They are what Raymond Williams would call a "residual" formation.[21]

George's brother the Ironmaster is a more complex figure. Like his son Watt, he is a "ghost" of the future, a member of the formation that Williams would call "emergent." Dynamic and plain-spoken, he represents the new industrial middle class that is seizing political and economic power from the old landed aristocracy. Attractive in many ways, he resembles one of Carlyle's Captains of Industry from *Past and Present*, and as such he has often been taken as the figure who represents Dickens's (and the novel's) best hope for the future. Seen from the perspective of *A Child's History*, however, the Ironmaster strikes me as a much less prepossessing figure. Although he has risen from the servant class, he is by no means a champion of the people in the tradition of Wat Tyler, Hampden, and Cromwell. Tough-minded and practical, he is a member of the new ruling elite, ready to take over from Sir Leicester and run the country. There is no indication that Rouncewell will have the people's interests at heart any more than Sir Leicester did. He will send his children (and their future wives) to Germany to be educated, just as Sir Leicester and his lady oriented themselves toward France and things French. If the Ironmaster is to be judged by the effects of industrialization on the English landscape, prospects for the nation's future seem bleak. The countryside through which George rides on his way to his brother's factory has been devastated. George leaves behind the green fields in the vicinity of Chesney Wold and comes upon "coal-pits and ashes, high chimneys and red bricks, blighted verdure, scorching fires, and a never-lightening cloud of smoke" (951). Although not exactly a Frankenstein's monster, the iron "ghost" of the Ironmaster leaves destruction in its wake. In historical terms the Ironmaster may turn out to be another repetition, in a different form, of the evils of the past. Whether Rouncewell will fight to preserve the people's liberties remains unclear. Dickens is uncertain and leaves the future open.

The ghosts who have the strongest claim on Dickens's allegiance in *Bleak House* are the ghosts of ordinary people. These include, but are not limited to, the ghosts of Nemo, Jo, and the Tom of Tom-all-Alone's. In these ghosts we find the clearest evidence of Dickens's radical populist sympathies, together with many of the qualities that Derrida evokes in his hauntology. Ghosts of the people are everywhere in *Bleak House*, although, as is often the way with ghosts, they are sometimes difficult to see. They make one of their earliest appearances, and in one of their favorite haunts, in chapter 22, when Bucket accompanies Mr. Snagsby down into the Dantean depths of Tom-all-Alone's in search of Jo.

> "Draw off a bit here, Mr. Snagsby," says Bucket, as a kind of shabby palanquin is borne towards them, surrounded by a noisy crowd. "Here's the fever coming up the street!"
>
> As the unseen wretch goes by, the crowd, leaving that object of attraction, hovers round the three visitors, like a dream of horrible faces, and fades away up alleys and into ruins, and behind walls; and with occasional cries and shrill whistles of warning, thenceforth flits about them until they leave the place. (358)

As Bucket and Snagsby wend their way back up toward the more reputable quarters of the city, the same crowd follows them "like a concourse of imprisoned demons, . . . yelling" (362).

Nemo is another ghost closely connected to the common people. Formerly a gentleman and a naval officer, now fallen upon harder times, he lives among the people and associates with the likes of Jo and Miss Flite, just as Lady Dedlock will later come to exchange her genteel identity for that of a common working-class woman. When Nemo dies, the unnamed present-tense narrator waxes indignant at the pauper's burial accorded to "our dear brother," and goes on to imagine the retribution that Nemo's ghost, manifest as disease emanating from his putrefying corpse and spreading through the "poisoned air," will exact on the rest of English society.

> With houses looking on, on every side, save where a reeking little tunnel of a court gives access to the iron gate—with every villainy of life in action close on death, and every poisonous element of death in action close on life—here, they lower our dear brother down a foot or two: here, sow him in corruption, to be raised in corruption: an avenging ghost at many a sick-bedside: a shameful testimony to future ages, how civilization and barbarism walked this boastful island together. (180)

A vengeful ghost from the past, rendered invisible by the process of corporeal decomposition, Nemo rises again from the dead in a grotesque parody of resurrection to infect the very air that circulates through the foggy streets of London. "Come, flame of gas, burning so sullenly above the iron gate, on which the poisoned air deposits its witch-ointment slimy to the touch! It is well that you should call to every passer-by, 'Look here!'" (180). A ghost of the past, he is very much a ghost of the present and of the future.

If Nemo, in the passages just quoted, is a synecdoche for all the nameless paupers buried in similar pestiferous London graveyards, his ghostly companion in wreaking vengeance on behalf of society's outcast members is the eponymous Tom who lends his name to the poorest district of the city.

> But [Tom] has his revenge. Even the winds are his messengers, and they serve him in these hours of darkness. There is not a drop of Tom's corrupted blood but propagates infection and contagion somewhere. It shall pollute, this very night, the choice stream (in which chemists on analysis would find the genuine nobility) of a Norman house, and his Grace shall not be able to say Nay to the infamous alliance. There is not an atom of Tom's slime, not a cubic inch of any pestilential gas in which he lives, not one obscenity or degradation about him, not an ignorance, not a wickedness, not a brutality of his committing, but shall work its retribution, through every order of society, up to the proudest of the proud, and to the

highest of the high. Verily, what with tainting, plundering, and spoiling, Tom has his revenge. (710)

The passage combines scientific and medical discourse with biblical rhetoric and metaphors of violent insurrection ("plunder," "spoil"). Tom, the people's ghost, is a force that barriers of class cannot restrain. We should remember that in his list of ten possible titles for the novel, the name "Tom-all-Alone's" figures in nine of them, before Dickens settled finally on *Bleak House*. Taken together, the list of titles names both the haunted house and the graveyard from which its ghosts arise.

Not all the people's ghosts in the novel are figures of revenge. Some merely stand and observe, like the allegorical figures of Ignorance and Want in *A Christmas Carol*. Such figures in *Bleak House* include the "dirty-faced little spectre" Peepy, who stares at Esther when she awakes at the end of chapter 4, and they include the pair of candles that she sees reflected in the window when she awakes at the start of chapter 8. They include the pair of Irish eyes that stare down at Nemo's corpse from the "discoloured shutters" in chapter 10: "Through the two gaunt holes pierced in them, famine might be staring in—the Banshee of the man upon the bed" (164).[22] They include the doll that hangs in the background of Krook's shop and looks out at us in the illustration "The appointed time." Even more sinister, they include the blackened effigy (another doll! Is it Esther's doll?) hanging from the eaves in the dark plate of "Tom-all-Alone's." Mute, invisible or nearly so, these are all versions of the ghost that Derrida says "looks at us and sees us not see it even when it is there." In their silent witnessing of death and scenes of immiseration or sometimes merely in their presence on other less notable occasions, these ghostly figures also make a claim for justice.

In their less ghostly incarnation, the poor sometimes speak for themselves, as the brickmaker does to Mrs. Pardiggle in chapter 8. His angry voice is one of the few instances in the novel of direct popular resistance to the controlling intrusions of middle-class hegemony, here in its religio-philanthropic mode. "Look at the water. Smell it! That's wot we drinks. How do you like it, and what do you think of gin, instead! An't my place dirty? Yes, it is dirty—it's nat'rally dirty, and it's nat'rally onwholesome; and we've had five dirty and onwholesome children, as is all dead infants, and so much the better for them, and for us besides" (132). More often than not, however, the poor are silent and unseen, excluded, as Jo is at the inquest, and forced to endure sanctimonious, hypocritical preaching, as Jo does at the hands of Mr. Chadband in chapter 25. Unable to speak for themselves, since they have no representation in Parliament, the ghostly poor are reduced to "yelling," like the crowd in Tom-all-Alone's, or else must rely on the voice of another, more articulate ghost, the unnamed present-tense narrator who serves as guide to half of the novel.

Earlier, I argued that *Bleak House* has two narrators, one inside the ghost story—Esther—and one outside. A more accurate characterization would be to say that both narrators are ghosts, but that each tells a different spectral story: one a story of psychological ghosts, the other a story of social and political haunting. The unnamed present-tense narrator always remains invisible. In cases where we cannot see the ghost, Derrida reminds us, "we must fall back on its voice." The unnamed present-tense narrator is pure voice and nothing else. Its voice is also the loudest and strongest in speaking out for justice. Nowhere is its demand for justice clearer than in the famous passage on the death of Jo: "Dead, your Majesty. Dead, my lords and gentlemen. Dead, Right Reverends and Wrong Reverends of every order. Dead, men and women, born with Heavenly compassion in your hearts. And dying thus around us, every day" (734). For Dickens, as for Hamlet (in Derrida's political reading of the play), "the time is out of joint." Like the ghost of Hamlet's father, the ghostly narrator summons those who rule England to "redress history, the *wrong* (tort) of history." If Her Majesty Queen Victoria is listening, this is her chance to prove that she deserves Dickens's praise of her as "very good" at the end of *A Child's History*.

If not the novel's final specter, Jo is—along with Guster—its most important historical ghost, and as such he rightly deserves his place of prominence on the novel's Vignette title page. Guster, we recall, is the final link between Lady Dedlock and Esther, the means by which the mother's letter begging forgiveness is transmitted to the daughter. In her exchange with Lady Dedlock, Guster is also the figure in and through whom the economy of the gift is most clearly evident: "She said she had nothing to give me, and I said I was poor myself and consequently wanted nothing. And so she said God bless you! And went" (912). Guster also has an important connection to Jo. Their exchange at the end of chapter 25 is another instance of what Derrida, citing Heidegger, calls the "gift without debt and without guilt." Guster is one of the few examples in the novel of genuine charity. "The charitable Guster," the ghostly narrator tells us,

> has her own supper of bread and cheese to hand to Jo; with whom she ventures to interchange a word or so, for the first time.
> "Here's something to eat, poor boy," says Guster.
> "Thank'ee, mum," says Jo.
> "Are you hungry?"
> "Jist!" says Jo.
> "What's gone of your father and your mother, eh?"
> Jo stops in the middle of a bite, and looks petrified. For this orphan charge of the Christian Saint whose shrine was at Tooting, has patted him on the shoulder; and it is the first time in his life that any decent hand has been so laid upon him. (415–16)

Guster performs true Christian charity, expecting no repayment and inducing no guilt. Jo receives the gift, frightened at his first experience of gentle kindness, but managing nevertheless to articulate in his own way the theme of justice. When asked if he is hungry, he replies: "Jist!"[23] Guster, we may also recall, is compared to "a popular ghost" (304). She is "popular," not in the sense of attracting widespread interest or appeal, but in representing the values and spirit of the "people"—the novel's ultimate source and standard of judgment.

Together with Guster, Jo is the novel's best embodiment of "popular" values. He too participates in the economy of the gift, exchanging thanks with Nemo's ghost by sweeping clean the graveyard step and uttering the simple words, "He wos wery good to me, he wos!" And, although he cannot quite manage to finish reciting the Lord's Prayer at Allan Woodcourt's prompting, he does participate, ever so slightly, in what Derrida calls the "emancipatory promise" of the ghost, its "messianic" or utopian dimension: "the coming of the other, the absolute and unpredictable singularity of the *arrivant as justice*." In Jo, we glimpse Derrida's "desire of resurrection. Re-naissance or *revenance?*"

In chapter 22, while on their visit to Tom-all-Alone's in search of Jo, Bucket and Snagsby come upon the brickmakers. One of the women has a baby, not three weeks old. Bucket shines his lantern on the infant, and Snagsby, another figure of charitable giving in the novel, "is strangely reminded of another infant, encircled with light, that he has seen in pictures" (360). Moments later, they spot Jo, and Bucket again shines his lantern: "Jo stands amazed in the disc of light, like a ragged figure in a magic lantern" (361–62). In the depths of Tom-all-Alone's, Bucket's lantern singles out two ghostly figures, both members of the lowest social order. One of them reminds Snagsby of the Christ child, though he does not use the name. The other is Jo, a magic lantern figure, but also in his way a Christian figure of Christian brotherhood. Jo is the absolute other of whom Levinas writes: "The relationship with the other is not an idyllic and harmonious relationship of communion, or a sympathy through which we put ourselves in the other's place; we recognize the other as resembling us, but exterior to us; the relationship with the other is a relationship with a Mystery."[24] Jo is the figure of absolute alterity to whom we must grant unconditional hospitality if we are to affirm our own humanity. Standing "amazed in the disc of light," Jo is a figure of amazement, our own as well as his. He is also Derrida's "messianism without religion, even a messianic without messianism, an idea of justice—which we distinguish from law or right and even from human rights." Very much a ghost of the present moment, of England in 1853, he is also the ghost of a time yet to come, the redemptive promise, or one of very few, in a book that manages at once to look deeply into the bleakness of England's darkest decade and to see glimmers of hope in a future that, as Esther Woodcourt also seems dimly to recognize, can only be supposed.[25]

EPILOGUE
Christmas

BLEAK HOUSE HAS NO CHRISTMAS CHAPTER. IT HAS NO DINGley Dell or other pastoral retreat to which the "good" characters can safely withdraw in midwinter or at novel's end to escape the social evils of contemporary English life. Even the Yorkshire establishment that Jarndyce sets up for Woodcourt and Esther at the end, which includes a little Growlery built specially for him, has dark corners and retains the ominous name of Bleak House. The closest the novel comes to depicting a happy communal meal is the "Old Girl's Birthday," celebrated by the Bagnet family in chapter 49, or perhaps, in a more grotesque mode, Volumnia's ghostly public assembly at the end of chapter 66. Chadband's greasy gourmandizing at the Snagsbys' in chapter 25 is the vulgar perversion of a Christian feast. Guster's willingness to share her bread with Jo at the end of the same chapter may be the novel's best example of genuine communion, but even it is a moment shared between two souls, not a communal celebration.

In December 1851, for the special extra Christmas issue of *Household Words,* Dickens wrote a short Christmas story, "What Christmas Is As We Grow Older." It is a melancholy piece, unlike his contribution for the previous year, "A Christmas Tree," though this too has a few dark moments. "What Christmas Is" is the first piece of Christmas prose that Dickens composed after the deaths of his father the previous March and his daughter Dora in April. It is small wonder that the story has a darker tone. Christmas was always for Dickens a time of reflection and introspection, of looking back at his own past and for meditating on the meaning of life more generally. Christmas was also a topic that he had made distinctly his own and that readers had come to identify with him and with his writing. "What Christmas Is" is also contemporary with the early composition of *Bleak House*. After delaying starting to work on it during the fall of 1851, Dickens had finally begun to write in November. The first monthly number appeared the following March. Although very different in tone and mood from his great novel, "What Christmas Is" has an interesting bearing on *Bleak House*. It belongs to the Shadowy World from which the novel emerged.

As its title suggests, "What Christmas Is As We Grow Older" presents the reflections of an older narrator, one who looks back on the Christmases of his youth and measures them against his present awareness of the passage of time and the absence of loved ones who, for one reason or another, cannot attend the annual gathering of family and friends.[1] The story begins with the evocation of a mythical time (*in illo tempore*) when Christmas made the world complete.

> Time was, with most of us, when Christmas Day encircling all our limited world like a magic ring, left nothing out for us to miss or seek; bound together all our home enjoyments, affections, and hopes; grouped everything and every one around the Christmas fire; and made the little picture shining in our bright young eyes, complete.[2]

The narrator knows that this magical timeless time was only an illusion, a picture shining in the eyes of childhood, and he juxtaposes it with the arrival, "all too soon," of a different experience of time, one marked by the absence of some special person or by one's own absence from the Christmas hearth.

> Time came, perhaps, all too soon, when our thoughts overleaped that narrow boundary; when there was some one (very dear, we thought then, very beautiful, and absolutely perfect) wanting to the fullness of our happiness; when we

were wanting too (or we thought so, which did just as well) at the Christmas hearth. (21)

The rest of the story (there is no real plot) takes the form of an extended meditation on the theme of presence and absence. The narrator remembers the Christmases of long ago (illusory but powerful and full of promise) and juxtaposes them with his knowledge of today (real but sad and full of nostalgia). He imagines what might have been but never was and sets this fantasy against what has been and still is, asking finally if life is little better than a dream.

His answer to this question is a resounding No! and he goes on to stress the value and importance of continuing to observe Christmas and to preserve the Christmas spirit, "which is the spirit of active usefulness, perseverance, cheerful discharge of duty, kindness and forbearance" (22). Although this may sound uncomfortably like Esther Summerson's vow of dutiful self-sacrifice, the narrator takes his meditations in a different direction. The greater his sense of loss, the greater his appreciation for the celebration that binds together those who remain. This is a theme that Dickens pursues elsewhere in his writing, most memorably for me in the homely piece of blacksmith poetry that Joe Gargery strikes off in chapter 27 of *Great Expectations*: "Life is made of ever so many partings welded together."[3] For the narrator of "What Christmas Is," the vivid realization of loss becomes the occasion for issuing a general invitation for everyone and everything within the circle of his life—past and present, real and imagined, friend and enemy—to join the feast. "Welcome, everything! Welcome, alike what has been, and what never was, and what we hope may be, to your shelter underneath the holly, to your places round the Christmas fire, where what is sits open-hearted!" (23). The best response to loss, the narrator asserts, is hospitality, an open-hearted welcome to every living thing. "On this day we shut out Nothing!" (23).

But "Pause," a different, graver voice commands, and then asks: "Nothing? Think!" What concerns the other voice here is whether the narrator is willing to open his invitation to "the shadow of a vast City where the withered leaves are lying deep . . . the shadow of the City of the Dead" (23). The narrator's answer to this question is once again affirmative, and he vows to welcome to his Christmas feast all the spirits of the dead. What follows and brings the story to a conclusion is the narrator's inventory of the ghosts whom he will include in his Christmas remembrance. The list is long and includes several generic types: a "poor mis-shapen boy" (recalling the *Carol*'s Tiny Tim) and a "gallant boy," presumably a soldier, fallen in some distant tropical land.

As it proceeds, however, the list grows increasingly personal, and one cannot help but think that Dickens is recalling lost figures from his own life. "There was a dear girl—almost a woman—never to be one—who made a mourning Christmas in a house of joy, and went her trackless way to the silent City" (24). Is this not Mary Hogarth? And when he thinks of "children angels that alight, so solemnly, so beautifully among the living children by the fire," it is difficult not to believe that Dora Annie Dickens is on his mind. The Dora reference becomes even more explicit when the narrator invokes the biblical story of the daughter of Jarius, whom Jesus raised from the dead and whose story is told in several of the Gospels. The list goes on: "Lost friend, lost child, lost parent, sister,[4] brother, husband, wife, we will not so discard you! You shall hold your cherished place in our Christmas hearts, and by our Christmas fires; and in the season of immortal hope, and on the birthday of immortal mercy, we will shut out Nothing!" (24–25).

The tone here is decidedly one of pathos, and the emphasis more explicitly Christian than one typically encounters in *Bleak House*. Nevertheless, I find an important similarity between story and novel in their shared concern with ghosts and hospitality. In both texts Dickens's social vision is inclusive. "We will shut out Nothing!" his narrator insists. What compensates for death, what redeems history and saves it from the endless bloody cycle of trauma and resistance, followed by repeated trauma, is the utopian vision offered by Christmas. It is easy to dismiss Dickens's "*Carol* philosophy" as soft sentimentalism and petit-bourgeois domestic ideology, cloaked in pseudoreligious romantic rhetoric and polished up for the holiday market, but such interpretations are too skeptical for my taste. I prefer a tougher-minded, though still tenderhearted, Dickens and a more generous reading of his Christmas spirit, one that is more radical and "popular" (in the same way that Guster is a

EPILOGUE   145

"popular ghost") and more closely aligned with the absolute or unconditional hospitality that Derrida posits as the ground of social justice.[5]

Here is how Dickens concludes "What Christmas Is":

> The winter sun goes down over town and village; on the sea it makes a rosy path, as if the Sacred tread were fresh upon the water. A few more moments, and it sinks, and night comes on, and lights begin to sparkle in the prospect. On the hill-side beyond the shapelessly-diffused town, and in the quiet keeping of the trees that gird the village-steeple, remembrances are cut in stone, planted in common flowers, growing in grass, entwined with lowly brambles around many a mound of earth. In town and village, there are doors and windows closed against the weather, there are flaming logs heaped high, there are joyful faces, there is healthy music of voices. Be all ungentleness and harm excluded from the temples of the Household Gods, but be those remembrances admitted with tender encouragement! They are of the time and all its comforting and peaceful reassurances; and of the history that reunited even upon earth the living and the dead; and of the broad beneficence and goodness that too many men have tried to tear to narrow shreds. (25)

This is not bourgeois domesticity only, but an expanded social vision of Christmas as a feast to which Jo and Nemo and Tom (of Tom-all-Alone's) and Guster and Lady Dedlock and Esther and Hampden and Wat Tyler and Dora (both of them) and John Dickens and Scrooge and Ignorance and Want and Marx and Derrida and Smike and you and I, dear reader, will be invited. And Micawber will make the punch.

APPENDIX
The Ghost in *Bleak House*

AM I THE ONLY ONE WHO THINKS HE'S SEEN THE GHOST IN *Bleak House?* I mean the ghost whose story Mrs. Rouncewell tells in chapter 7 and whose footsteps echo across the Ghost's Walk terrace at Chesney Wold. So far as I know, no one else has ever claimed to see the ghost—no reader or critic, no character in the novel, not even the unnamed present-tense narrator. People hear the ghost, or what they take to be the sound of its steps on the terrace, drip, drip, drip; but no one sees the ghost. I do.

My friend Bob Newsom, a distinguished Dickensian and expert reader of *Bleak House,* insists that I'm hallucinating. What I read as "ghost," Bob says is merely shadow. But he tells me not to worry. *Bleak House* does this sort of thing to people, he says, excites their imagination, plays tricks on the eye and ear, makes them see things that aren't there, shadows that move, optical illusions. If I really want to explain myself, Bob continues, all I need to do is tell my story, how I first thought I saw a ghost, but then came to realize the error of my ways. I can then chalk the whole experience up to "the *Bleak House* effect," the novel's way of luring its characters (and its readers) to imagine things that might have been but never were or that exist only in their minds.

Bob may be right. I may be like Esther Summerson when she first sees Lady Dedlock in the church and suddenly has visions of her godmother and her own younger self; or like Mrs. Snagsby, projecting her suspicions onto every new bit of information and inventing evidence to fit her suspicions; or like Mr. Guppy in chapter 33. When the servant leaves him in the dimly lit library of the house in town for his first interview with Lady Dedlock, "Mr. Guppy looks into the shade in all directions, discovering everywhere a certain charred and whitened little heap of coal or wood. Presently he hears a rustling. Is it—? No, it's no ghost; but fair flesh and blood, most brilliantly dressed" (533). As Guppy waits for his appointment, the burnt remains of Krook linger in his memory, but it is Lady Dedlock herself, not a ghost, who appears out of the shadows. Although I've witnessed no recent scenes of spontaneous combustion, "my" ghost may be something similar—the product of an overactive imagination, wishful thinking, or something I ate. But I'm not easily dissuaded. I know the ghost is there. I still see it, and I think others do too. They just don't recognize it. You decide.

When I say I see the ghost, I mean I see it in one of the novel's illustrations: "The Mausoleum at Chesney Wold" (see fig. 9 on p. 81). The figure I identify as the ghost is standing (or hovering) in front of the mausoleum door on the viewer's right-hand side, just inside the fence that surrounds the vault and immediately to the left of the piece of statuary that guards the entrance to the plot. Darker than the surrounding area, but not so dark as the shadow just above it cast by the curved balustrade that leads up to the mausoleum door, the figure is nevertheless transparent. Behind and through it, the surface of the door is visible. Roughly triangular in shape and slightly wider as it nears the ground, the figure is surmounted by a small oval, lighter in color, that I read as its face, though no features are discernible. The "face" may be covered by a veil. The figure's "body" is draped in something that resembles a long, loose-fitting gown or cloak of the sort worn out of doors by Lady Dedlock and Esther in the novel's other illustrations. This "gown" could also be a sheet or shroud. Judging from this "garment," I would say the figure is a woman. Judging by the door behind it, I would say the figure is of an appropriate human size and scale.

Why has no one ever commented on the strange figure—or, if you prefer, the ambiguous patch of darkness—that I read as a ghost? One reason is that many modern editions of the novel either do not contain a full set of the original Hablot K. Browne ("Phiz") illustrations or else have reproductions of poor quality. To see the ghost, you need a good edition, and you need to know where to look. Another reason readers have not recognized the ghost is that the verbal text makes no mention of one. "The Mausoleum at Chesney Wold" corresponds to a passage near the beginning of chapter 66 in the novel's final double monthly number. The passage in question describes Lady Dedlock's final resting place in the Dedlock family mausoleum and, in particular, the regular visits faithfully paid by Sir Leicester to the site of his wife's grave. Here is the passage.

> Up from among the fern in the hollow, and winding by the bridle-road among the trees, comes sometimes to this lonely spot the sound of horses' hoofs. Then may be seen Sir Leicester—invalided, bent, and almost blind, but of a worthy presence yet—riding with a stalwart man beside him, constant to his bridle-rein. When they come to a certain spot before the mausoleum door, Sir Leicester's accustomed horse stops of his own accord, and Sir Leicester, pulling off his hat, is still for a few moments before they ride away. (981)

Told by the unnamed present-tense narrator, this brief paragraph moves in three sentences from a slightly spooky evocation of approaching sound to a description of the two visitors, Sir Leicester and the stalwart George, to their halt at a particular spot before the mausoleum, and finally to their departure.

There's no ghost in this passage, right? Just Sir Leicester and George Rouncewell. But wait—the passage contains two details that are worth another look: the mausoleum door and Sir Leicester's failing eyesight. If there were anyone or anything in front of the door, it might well escape Sir Leicester's notice, since he is "almost blind." Is it possible that the text is telling us to look for something that Sir Leicester does not see and to look for it in the vicinity of the door?

Readers of illustrated novels—and this includes most literary critics—tend to privilege the verbal text. They regard illustrations as secondary, as the transposition into visual terms of words on the page. Such readers seldom stop to consider the possibility that a visual image might have priority, might tell us something that the words omit or only suggest, or, alternatively, that verbal text and illustration may tell conflicting stories. In this connection, it is useful to recall an illustration from the final chapter of Thackeray's *Vanity Fair* (1847–48). In "Becky's second appearance in the character of Clytemnestra," the figure of Becky Sharp, holding what might be a dagger or perhaps a vial of poison, appears, heavily shaded, hidden behind a curtain and looking out at a helpless Jos Sedley (fig. 11). Although Becky had taken the part of Clytemnestra during the charades enacted earlier in the novel, there is no mention in the verbal text of any second appearance by her in this role. Text and image tell different stories. If we privilege the verbal text, then the image may be an illusion, Jos's hallucination or a trap set for the suspicious reader who wants to think the worst of Becky. If we privilege the illustration, Becky is a murderess. In either case, the image of Becky behind the curtain, looking sinister, is unquestionably there and is confirmed by the illustration's caption, whereas the presence of a figure of any sort in the illustration from *Bleak House* remains in doubt. Did Browne know the Thackeray illustration? Probably. Was he doing something similar at the end of *Bleak House*? Perhaps. Did Dickens have anything to do with it? We don't know.

"The Mausoleum at Chesney Wold" is one of four illustrations that Browne executed for the final double monthly number of *Bleak House,* dated September 1853. Of the other three images, two were meant for the novel's front matter when it was eventually published in volume form: the frontispiece (a dark plate of Chesney Wold) and the vignette title page (an image of Jo the crossing sweeper). The third image corresponds to a passage in chapter 64 and shows Mr. Guppy's second proposal to Esther. "The Mausoleum at Chesney Wold" corresponds to a passage in the novel's penultimate chapter, "Down in Lincolnshire." It is thus the novel's final illustration, or at least the one that accompanies the passage closest to the end of the novel's verbal text. As such, it occupies an important position in the sequence of illustrations and can be taken, in a certain sense, as part of the novel's ending—the final visual image with which the reader is left.

In a letter to Browne, dated June 29, 1853, and mailed from Boulogne, where he had gone to finish the last two monthly numbers of

FIG. 11. William Makepeace Thackeray, "Becky's second appearance in the character of Clytemnestra," etching from *Vanity Fair: A Novel without A Hero*, 1848. (Courtesy of the Department of Special Collections, Stanford University Libraries)

Bleak House, Dickens wrote to say that he would soon be sending his directions for the final four illustrations of the novel. "I am now ready with four subjects for the concluding double No. and will post them to you tomorrow or next day!!!!!!!!!!!!" (*Letters* 7: 107). Regrettably, the subsequent letter containing those instructions has not survived; we therefore have no information about Dickens's wishes in this respect, other than the fact that he did have such wishes and presumably communicated them to Browne. But what about Browne? What do we know or what can we surmise about his intentions?

The only evidence of Browne's plans, aside from the final illustration itself, is to be found in two drawings, one in the Free Library of Philadelphia (in the Elkins collection) and the other in the Beinecke Library at Yale (in the Gimbel collection). Both are of interest, though neither settles the question of whether Browne (and/or Dickens) meant there to be a ghost in the final illustration.

The Elkins drawing (fig. 12) is what Michael Steig calls a "working drawing."[1] That is, it is the drawing that Browne used in order to transfer the image from paper to the steel plate prior to etching. As such, the drawing is a mirror image of the final illustration. Browne would place a tracing of the drawing face down over the waxed plate, pass the plate through the press so that the marks of the drawing were transferred to the ground, remove the paper, and complete the image directly on the plate using his needle.[2] He would then bathe the plate in an acid solution, allowing the acid to eat into the plate where the lines were drawn. The resulting plate could then be inked and used to print the final illustration.

In the Elkins drawing, the place where my ghost should appear is on the left-hand side; when printed, this becomes the viewer's right. I would very much like to say that I see a figure there, but the most I can claim is that the space is somewhat blurry, especially in comparison to the opposite side, where the door panels are clearly visible and nothing blocks our view. The Elkins drawing contains another curious feature, however. Three little demons or goblin-like figures appear in its margins. One thumbs his nose, another smirks and holds a curved pipelike object in his hand, and a third peers intently into the center of the image. The technical term for such marginal figures is "remarques." What are we to make of them?

Steig, Jane R. Cohen, and Valerie Browne Lester all mention these demons and suggest that they reveal something about Browne's attitude toward Dickens, a mocking independence perhaps.[3] My own suggestion is that the demons hint at the presence of other spirits and that the demon on the upper right, the one with the bulging eyes, is staring at

THE GHOST IN BLEAK HOUSE

something that Sir Leicester, whose viewpoint the illustration presumably represents, cannot see. A mausoleum, after all, is a logical place for ghosts to appear, and if humans cannot see them, perhaps other spirits can. We know that Chesney Wold is supposed to have a family ghost and that characters hear what they think are its footsteps on the terrace. If a ghost haunts the house (and if other ghostly figures, such as Volumnia and even Esther, do so at various points in the novel), why should a ghost not also appear at the spot where Lady Dedlock is buried?

The Gimbel drawing (fig. 13) complicates these speculations. Unlike

FIG. 12. Hablot K. Browne, "The Mausoleum at Chesney Wold," working drawing, *Bleak House,* 1853. (Used by permission of the Rare Book Department, Free Library of Philadelphia)

the Elkins drawing, it is not a mirror image of the final illustration. As such, it may be what Steig calls a "preliminary sketch," one that Browne produced in advance of making the plate as a guide for himself to what the final image would look like when it appeared in the novel. More likely, in view of the drawing's high degree of finish (which in turn suggests a more leisurely composition than the short turnaround time needed to complete four plates for the final number would have allowed), it is a subsequent, extra-illustrated drawing, one that Browne produced after the novel was published to use as a gift or as a record for himself or to sell to a collector. Signed "Phiz" in the lower left-hand corner and with the notation "BH" in the upper left, this drawing is much more finished than the Elkins image. Done in two different colors of ink and heightened with a white wash to suggest the reflection of light on the surface of the mausoleum, this drawing recalls similar fancy extra-illustrations that Browne produced after the fact from plates he made for other novels.

In any event, whether executed before the Elkins sketch or after Browne's final etching for the novel was complete, the Gimbel drawing does not support my "ghost" hypothesis. No figure stands before the mausoleum door. The blurry space in the Elkins sketch is gone. In the Gimbel drawing, that space is unambiguously vacant. Moreover, and somewhat curiously, there is no trace of the shadows that appear in the final image. Despite these facts, the Gimbel drawing does not prove conclusively—beyond the shadow of a doubt, I am tempted to say—that no ghost is present in the final illustration. Browne could have added the ghost at the last minute, directly onto the plate. Steig argues that Browne made such changes in other illustrations, adding details that do not appear in the working drawings and even sometimes reversing the direction in which a figure faces.[4] In order to confirm or disprove the presence of my "ghost," we must return to the final illustration as it appears in a good first edition of the novel.

Finding a "good first edition" of *Bleak House* is not as easy as it might at first appear. Illustrations in the original serial parts vary tremendously in quality. As more copies of the parts were printed, the plates from which the illustrations were taken began to wear, and the images themselves deteriorated accordingly.[5] Another difficulty arises

FIG. 13. Hablot K. Browne, "The Mausoleum at Chesney Wold," drawing, *Bleak House,* 1853? (Courtesy of the Beinecke Rare Book and Manuscript Library, Yale University)

from differences in inking between one impression and the next. More heavily inked plates produce darker images, with a resulting loss of clarity and sharpness of detail. Moreover, at a certain point, the novel's publishers, Bradbury and Evans, began printing Browne's images using lithography, a technique in which the original designs were copied onto stone with a greasy material, allowing printed impressions to be taken from them. In an undated letter to Dickens, Browne complained of the ruinous effect that lithography had on his plates for *Bleak House*. "I am told," he writes, "that from 15 to 25,000 [copies] are monthly printed from lithographic transfers—some of these impressions, when the etching is light and sketchy, will pass muster with the uninitiated—but, the more elaborate the etching—the more villainous the transfer."[6] The "villainous" effect of lithographic transfers may have affected some of the novel's "dark plates," of which "The Mausoleum at Chesney Wold" is an example.[7] Whether the result of wear, poor inking, or lithography, fine details in the plates are often lost. In some monthly parts of *Bleak House*, the space in front of the mausoleum door becomes entirely black, and the shadows cast by the entrance balustrade, along with any figure that might be there, are swallowed up in undifferentiated inky darkness (fig. 14).

A different problem appears in some later editions of the novel, such as the Nonesuch.[8] These editions use worn (or in some cases, perhaps retouched) plates, with the result that the shape I read as a ghost appears not as a patch of darkness, but as a lighter figure that stands out against a darker background (fig. 15). The result is an even more "ghostly" effect, since the figure now seems to possess the more conventional attributes of a phantom: an eerie glow and even greater transparency. Although striking in appearance—and providing evidence, some might argue, for the existence of an earlier figure occupying this position and of which it is the trace—this "ghost" may be the misleading result of a worn or reworked plate, since in the earliest impressions the "figure," if it exists, should be dark.

It is also possible that the ambiguous patch of darkness I identify as "ghost" may be an artifact of reprinting, an effect of mechanical reproduction rather than part of Browne's original design. While it would certainly be gratifying to know what Browne (and Dickens) intended in this regard, from another perspective their "authorial" intention ultimately matters less than the fact that some copies of the original serial parts do contain the shadowy presence that resembles a human figure. I confess that I take a certain pleasure in the thought that some copies con-

FIG. 14. Hablot K. Browne, "The Mausoleum at Chesney Wold," lithographic transfer?, *Bleak House*, 1853, first bound edition. (Author's personal collection)

tain this shadow or figure and some do not. It is often the way of ghosts to come and go mysteriously. Moreover, they do not appear to everyone.

"The Mausoleum at Chesney Wold" and the accompanying passage from chapter 66 recall the conclusion to another Dickens novel, one in which the prospect of ghostly visitation is explicitly mentioned. The final paragraph of *Oliver Twist* describes the visit to a village church where

FIG. 15. Hablot K. Browne, "The Mausoleum at Chesney Wold," etching from *Bleak House,* 1938 ed. (rpt. 2005, Nonesuch edition). (Used by permission of Duckworth Publishers)

a marble tablet bearing the name "Agnes" commemorates Oliver's dead mother. Although the church contains no coffin and no corpse, the narrative voice suggests that the spirit of Agnes will return to visit that spot.

> Within the altar of the old village church, there stands a white marble tablet, which bears as yet but one word,—'Agnes!'

THE GHOST IN BLEAK HOUSE

There is no coffin in that tomb; and may it be many, many years, before another name is placed above it! But, if the spirits of the Dead ever come back to earth, to visit spots hallowed by the love—the love beyond the grave—of those whom they knew in life, I believe that the shade of Agnes sometimes hovers round that solemn nook.[9]

The accompanying illustration by Cruikshank shows Oliver and Rose Maylie standing inside the church and looking at the tablet (fig. 16). There

FIG. 16. George Cruikshank, "Rose Maylie and Oliver," etching from *Oliver Twist,* 1838. (Courtesy of the Department of Special Collections, Stanford University Libraries)

is no hint of a ghost in the illustration, but the novel's final paragraph invites the reader/viewer to imagine one "hovering" nearby. Is it possible that when he wrote the story of another illegitimate child who yearns for the presence of a mother who dies, a story in which ghosts and ghostly presences abound, Dickens may have reverted to the idea with which his earlier novel ended and instructed his illustrator to suggest the presence of a "shade" lingering near the site where the mother is buried?

In their study of first editions of Dickens's novels, Thomas Hatton and Arthur Cleaver report having examined a thousand sets of original serial parts of *Bleak House.* In my research, I have consulted only a dozen, yet among these I can report considerable variation in the quality of the mausoleum illustration. Of the examples I have seen, and in support of my contention that some of them contain the figure of a ghost, I have selected and reproduced here as figure 9 the impression that I consider the best in terms of its overall clarity and sharpness of line. I see a shade. Bob sees only shadow. What do you see?

NOTES

1. VOICE

1. Other *Bleak House* essays by scholars associated in one way or another with the Dickens Project include those by Budd, Daleski, Eigner, Fletcher, Gilbert, Hack, Hochman, D. A. Miller, Hillis Miller, Sadrin, and Vanden Bossche. The *Bleak House* bibliography is immense. Among the many studies focusing on Esther Summerson, I have found especially useful those by Cummings, Graver, Peltason, Sternlieb, Welsh, and Wilt.

2. Dever draws especially on Lacan's "Seminar on 'The Purloined Letter'" and Winnicott's "Transitional Objects and Transitional Phenomena." To these I would add André Green's essay "The Dead Mother." See chapter 3 below.

3. Dever, *Death and the Mother*, 84; emphasis in the original.

4. Dickens, *Bleak House*, 580. All further references to the text are to the 2003 Penguin Classics edition and are cited parenthetically by page number.

5. Dever, *Death and the Mother*, 84.

6. Welsh attempts to distinguish between the two positions by calling the narrator "Summerson" and the protagonist "Esther," but acknowledges that "this distinction is bound to blur" (*Dickens Redressed*, 19). In my analysis I have attempted to maintain the distinction by using present-tense verbs ("Esther writes," "Esther reports") for the retrospective narrator and past-tense verbs for actions performed by her younger self, but even this strategy is bound to fail.

7. Brooks, *Reading for the Plot*, 97.

8. Newsom (*Dickens on the Romantic Side*) was the first to emphasize the importance of the uncanny in *Bleak House;* his discussion remains an invaluable starting point for any subsequent analysis. See also Herbert, "Occult in *Bleak House*."

9. We should not overlook the tripling in Esther's characteristic self-admonition. For a penetrating discussion of the tension between knowing and not knowing in Dickens, see Bodenheimer, *Knowing Dickens*, especially chapter 3. Bodenheimer does not discuss Esther, although much of her analysis has direct relevance to my argument here and elsewhere.

10. The phrase appears in Forster's *Life of Charles Dickens*, 1:15. Dickens uses different variants of it in his own writing. For the history of this phrase, which had been used previously by other writers, see Sicher, *Rereading the City*, 50–51.

11. I take the term "unclaimed experience" from Caruth. See chapter 3 below.

12. Hillis Miller makes an early and influential argument along these lines in his 1958 book on Dickens, *Charles Dickens: The World of His Novels*. Similar readings of Esther, although with a different emphasis, tend to dominate in most "political" or ideological readings of the novel.

13. On Esther's "confusion," see especially Wilt, "Confusion and Consciousness."

14. For a different reading of "Summerson," see Sadrin, "Charlotte Dickens."

15. My discussion of voice relies heavily on the work of Gérard Genette. For Genette, voice refers to those determinations "dealing with the way in which the narrating itself is implicated in the narrative, narrating in the sense in which I have defined it, that is, the narrative situation or its instance, and along with its two protagonists: the narrator and his audience, real or implied" (*Narrative Discourse*, 31). Also useful for their emphasis on voice as a sign of the physical body are Barthes, "Grain of the Voice"; Leonardi and Pope, *Diva's Mouth*; and Connor, *Dumbstruck*. See also Brau, *La voix narrative*. For a reading of Chaucer's Wife of Bath along lines similar to my discussion of Esther Woodcourt, see Leicester, *Disenchanted Self*, especially 89–91.

16. For a very different reading of this passage, one that explicitly rejects the idea of trauma, see Case, "Gender and History."

17. Dever, *Death and the Mother*, 93.

18. The lodge where Esther and her mother meet is first mentioned in chapter 2: "My Lady Dedlock (who is childless), looking out in the early twilight from her boudoir at a keeper's lodge, and seeing . . . a child, chased by a woman, running out into the rain to meet the shining figure of a wrapped-up man coming through the gate, has been quite put out of temper" (21). In addition to sounding the mother-daughter theme that will unfold gradually in the following chapters, this passage hints obliquely at the possibility of a father as well. The wet and wrapped-up, "shining" (here read "ghostly") male figure "coming through the gate" anticipates Hawdon/Nemo, buried behind the iron gate of a London graveyard. There is a further sad irony in the phrase "keeper's lodge." When it comes to children, Lady Dedlock is anything but a "keeper." Note that at the end of the book, George (the prodigal son now reunited with his mother) ends up living in the Keeper's lodge at Chesney Wold—"Keeper" here with a capital letter (982).

19. Newsom, Kaplan, Frank, Stewart, Peltason, and Dever all note the strangeness of this passage and comment on it.

20. Bollas, *Shadow of the Object*, 3–4, 210, 235.

21. West, "Esther's Illness," 31.

22. I use the term here in the sense that André Green gives to it. See chapter 3 below.

23. The enigmatic paragraph in chapter 31 may well be part of the "great turning idea" that Dickens refers to in a letter written as he was completing monthly number 10. On November 19, 1852, he wrote to Angela Burdett Coutts, "I have been so busy, leading up to the great turning idea of the Bleak House story, that I have lived this last week or ten days in a perpetual scald and boil" (*Letters*, ed. Storey, Tillotson, and Burgis, Pilgrim Edition, 6:805). All further references to Dickens's letters are to the Pilgrim Edition and will be cited parenthetically by volume and page number. Critics have offered different suggestions as to what this "turning idea" might be. See, for example, Slater, *Charles Dickens*, 347–48 and 652, n11. In my reading, Esther's unconscious recognition of her mother's identity and her consequent disfigurement are the great turning idea of the story.

2. ILLUSTRATION

1. Valuable discussions of Dickens and Phiz and of the *Bleak House* illustrations in particular can be found in Steig, *Dickens and Phiz*, 131–58; Cohen, *Dickens and His Original Illustrators*, 107–14; Harvey, *Victorian Novelists and Their Illustrators*, 151–57; and Stein, "*Bleak House* and Illustration" and "Dickens and Illustration." The critic who comes closest to addressing the issues of perspective that I discuss in this chapter is Patten in his excellent essay "Serial Illustration and Storytelling," especially 96–102. Although he accurately emphasizes the "staggering" ontological and epistemological complexities of Phiz's effort to represent simultaneously David's child and adult perspectives as well as the external viewpoint of the "author," Patten retains the older critical term "point of view," whereas I prefer the narratological term "focalization."

2. Bal, *Narratology*, 142–70.

3. For a valuable overview of Bal's "rhetorical" approach to the study of visual culture and for a discussion of her debt to Benveniste in particular, see Bryson, "Art and Intersubjectivity," 1–39.

4. Some may argue that Jo is pointing at Nemo's grave, not at the rat, and indeed the text does state that he points initially at the spot where Nemo is buried: "Over yinder. Among them piles of bones, and close to that there kitchin winder!" (262). I contend, however, that he has been distracted from the grave by the sudden appearance of a rat on the other side of the burial ground; in the illustration he points away from the kitchen window, which is visible to the viewer's left, and thus away from the grave, not toward it.

5. The orientation of Esther's body in this illustration is ambiguous. Her lower body can be read as facing in either direction, recalling the famously undecidable duck-rabbit figure from Gestalt psychology. Her flowing skirt makes it impossible to read the exact position of her hips, and her upper body is posed so as prevent the viewer from knowing which of her shoulders is closer to the picture plane. However, the heavy diagonal fold lines in her skirt suggest, without giving definitive proof, that she is twisting her body away from Ada and toward Miss Flite.

6. I am grateful to my former student, Nick Evans, for drawing my attention to the significance of this tree and the ambiguous action being performed beneath it to the rear.

7. The figure of the tree reappears with ominous meaning in the description of the portrait of Lady Dedlock that hangs over the chimneypiece at Chesney Wold: "And now, upon my lady's picture over the great chimneypiece, a weird shade falls from some old tree, that turns it pale, and flutters it, and looks as if a great arm held a veil or hood, watching an opportunity to draw it over her" (641).

8. Is there perhaps an unconscious play on words in the kind of flowers Esther names? Charley gathers "violets." Her flower gathering may also suggest a link to the myth of Proserpine, discussed in chapter 3 below.

9. Bal, *Narratology*, 164.

3. PSYCHOANALYSIS

1. For psychoanalysis, see Laplanche, "Notes on Afterwardsness." For narratology, see Brooks, "Fictions of the Wolfman: Freud and Narrative Understanding," in *Reading for the Plot*, 264–85; and Culler, "Story and Discourse." For epistemology, see Lukacher, *Primal Scenes*.

2. Abraham and Torok, *Shell and the Kernel*, 171–76.

3. Stolorow and Atwood, *Contexts of Being*, 54.

4. Caruth, *Unclaimed Experience*, 4. Subsequent references are cited parenthetically by page number.

5. Green, "Dead Mother," 142. Subsequent references are cited parenthetically by page number.

6. For greater accuracy and in order to allow for the possibility of a female infant, I have substituted ungendered pronouns in these passages for the masculine "him" and "himself" of the English translation.

7. Freud, "Mourning and Melancholia," 170.

8. Frank interestingly suggests that what Esther sees reflected back to her is a Medusa's head and that she "in effect turns herself to stone" (*Dickens and the Romantic Self*, 116).

9. *Bleak House*, ed. Ford and Monod, Norton Critical Edition, 855, n456.19.

10. Frank (*Dickens and the Romantic Self*, 117–21) gives an excellent discussion of Esther's journey into the unconscious, drawing on the existential

psychology of Rollo May, but pays little attention to Bucket's role in the process or to Esther's place as retrospective narrator of these events.

4. ENDINGS

1. I am grateful to Hilary Schor, who first called this detail to my attention.

2. For a thoughtful, sensitive discussion of the novel's ending, see Torgovnick, *Closure in the Novel,* 37–60. Her analysis and mine have some similarities, though we arrive at quite different conclusions.

3. Peltason, "Esther's Will," 673, 688.

4. "Inexpressible mourning erects a secret tomb inside the subject. Reconstituted from the memories of words, scenes, and affects, the objectal correlative of the loss is buried alive in the crypt as a full-fledged person, complete with its own topography" (Abraham and Torok, *Shell and the Kernel,* 130).

5. In this connection it is worth noting that the verb "to suppose" is one of the key terms in the lexicon of Jacques Derrida—most famously, perhaps, at the outset of his essay "Le Facteur de la verité" ("The Purveyor of Truth"), which begins: "La psychanalyse, à supposer, se trouve." See also chapter 6 below.

6. During the early 1850s, the word "supposing" also carried a political significance for Dickens. In 1850–51 he wrote and published in *Household Words* four short articles entitled "Supposing" in which he challenged various aspects of the existing social and political order and imagined alternate, usually utopian, possibilities. I am grateful to Nirshan Perera for calling these to my attention.

7. Whether a human figure of any kind is visible in this illustration remains a matter of speculation. For a rehearsal of the evidence and of my reasons for believing such a figure to be present, see the appendix.

8. Quoted in Lester, *Phiz,* 154.

9. In *Paperwork,* 80–92, Kevin McLaughlin gives an excellent discussion of the importance of paper in *Bleak House,* but says nothing about ink. For an elegant analysis of ink and writing in the novel, with an emphasis on problems of signification, see Ragussis, "Ghostly Signs."

10. I am tempted to propose yet another internal focalizer of this scene, Dickens himself as he stood before the Vault in which his daughter Dora was initially interred. See chapter 5 below.

5. DICKENS

1. Bodenheimer, *Knowing Dickens,* 55–89. On implicit or "procedural" as opposed to explicit or "declarative" memory, see Siegel, *Developing Mind,* 27–66.

2. Dickens, *David Copperfield,* 11.

3. On Saturday, June 11, 1853, recovering from an illness that had kept him "six days in bed, for the first time in my life," Dickens wrote to Lady Eastlake as follows: "Since Monday last, I have been shaving a man every morning—a

stranger to me—with big gaunt eyes and a hollow cheek—whose appearance was rather irksome and oppressive. I am happy to say he has at last retired from the looking-glass, and is replaced by the familiar personage whom I have lathered and scraped these twenty years" (*Letters,* 7:95). To Bradbury and Evans on the same day, he wrote that he was "much stronger" and was "fast getting back my old face" (96). The scene in which Esther first looks in the mirror after recovering from her illness occurs in chapter 36, published in monthly number 12 (February 1853).

4. Mamie Dickens, *My Father,* 47–49.

5. For these and other biographical and historical allusions in the novel, Susan Shatto's *Companion to "Bleak House"* is invaluable. Shatto finds "no evidence to support the suggestion that Mrs. Rouncewell is modeled on Dickens's paternal grandmother," however (75).

6. For a fuller interpretation along these lines, see Jordan, "Social Sub-text."

7. See Kaplan, *Mesmerism,* 113–18, for a relevant discussion of how mirrors and similar bright objects were used in inducing mesmeric trances.

8. Hillis Miller, Introduction to *Bleak House.*

9. Bodenheimer, *Knowing Dickens,* 16.

10. Dickens, *Speeches,* 122.

11. Mamie Dickens, "Dickens at Home," 38.

12. Forster, *Life,* 2:206; emphasis in the original.

13. Friedman, *Dickens's Fiction,* 77–94.

14. In writing these words, Dickens seems almost to be laying down a "track" that can be followed, daring "any one," any reader, to assume the role of Detective Bucket and "trace" the deserted infant to its source.

15. For a perceptive analysis of insideness and outsideness in the novel's two narrators, but with a different emphasis from mine, see Buzard, *Disorienting Fiction,* 105–56.

6. SPECTERS

1. Tracy, "Lighthousekeeping"; Andrew Miller, *Novels behind Glass;* Carlisle, "Crystal Palace."

2. Wilkinson, "From Faraday to Judgment Day"; Lai, "Victorian Science."

3. D. A. Miller, *Novel and the Police,* 58–106.

4. Schor, *Daughter of the House,* 101–23.

5. Vanden Bossche, "Class Discourse and Popular Agency."

6. Ghosts in *Bleak House* have come in for a good bit of critical discussion. See Newsom, *Dickens on the Romantic Side;* Arac, *Commissioned Spirits;* Friedman, "Considerate Ghost"; and especially Herbert, "Occult in *Bleak House.*"

7. *David Copperfield,* 1.

8. *David Copperfield,* 8.

9. On Dickens and sanitary reform, with special attention to graveyards (but not to Dora's grave), see Fielding and Brice, "*Bleak House* and the Graveyard."

10. An example, perhaps, of the cross-generational transmission of trauma discussed by Abraham and Torok.

11. *A Child's History* appeared serially (but according to no fixed schedule) in *Household Words*, beginning on January 25, 1851, and concluding on December 10, 1853. Two excellent discussions of *A Child's History*, to which I am indebted, are by Jann, "Fact, Fiction, and Interpretation," and Lucas, "Past and Present." See also Gardiner, "Uses of History," and Birch, "Forgotten Book."

12. Collins, *Dickens and Education*, 63.

13. *"Master Humphrey's Clock" and "A Child's History of England,"* 149. Subsequent page references are to this edition and will be noted parenthetically in the text with the abbreviation *CHE*.

14. A more direct verbal echo of Krook's spontaneous combustion comes in Dickens's strange description of the auto-incineration of a group of twelfth-century Jews under the leadership of one Jocen. Trapped and threatened with violence by a group of angry Christians, the Jews decide to destroy themselves rather than die at the hands of their enemies. "They made a blazing heap of all their valuables, and, when those were consumed, set the castle in flames. While the flames roared and crackled around them, and shooting up into the sky, turned it blood-red, Jocen cut the throat of his beloved wife, and stabbed himself. All others who had wives or children, did the like dreadful deed. When the populace broke in, they found (except the trembling few, cowering in corners, whom they soon killed) only heaps of greasy cinders, with here and there something like part of the blackened trunk of a burnt tree, but which had lately been a human creature, formed by the beneficent hand of the Creator as they were" (*CHE* 224).

15. Two comments by a Dickensian of the 1950s are instructive in helping to understand the significance of the English Civil War for Dickens and his contemporaries. "The Reformation and the struggle between Charles the First and Parliament . . . were examples of two causes which Dickens as a Liberal held especially dear—the struggle against religious intolerance, and the struggle against autocratic despotism. . . . One must remember that the Civil War loomed extremely large in Dickens's historical horizon. He cannot speak of a strike at Manchester without bringing Hampden's name into it. I think one can say that he and the people of his generation regarded the conflict as a social revolution, and not merely as a political and economic struggle as we do to-day" (Birch, "Forgotten Book," 155–56).

16. On the difference between Macaulay's "Whig" vision of English history and Dickens's more "Radical" perspective, see the excellent discussion by Lucas ("Past and Present"), one of the very few critics to draw a connection between *A Child's History* and *Bleak House*. On Dickens and popular radicalism in general and on some of its implications for *Bleak House*, see Ledger, *Popular Radical Imagination*. Ledger does not discuss *A Child's History*.

17. Lucas, "Past and Present," 149.

18. Invoking Derrida, Hilary Schor calls for a hauntological reading of *Bleak House*, but she does not attempt to provide one (*Daughter of the House*, 108).

19. Derrida, *Specters of Marx*, xviii; emphasis in the original. Subsequent references are cited parenthetically by page number.

20. See Sucksmith, "Dedlock, Wat Tyler, and the Chartists." A Chartist Wat Tyler League and Wat Tyler Brigade existed.

21. Williams, *Marxism and Literature*, 121–27.

22. Bigelow (*Fiction, Famine*, 91) draws the connection between this passage and the Irish famine. The Banshee is a Celtic ghost.

23. For this lovely insight, I am indebted to John Bowen.

24. Levinas, *Time and the Other*, 75.

25. "Once again, here as elsewhere, wherever deconstruction is at stake, it would be a matter of linking an *affirmation* (in particular a political one), *if there is any*, to the experience of the impossible, which can only be a radical experience of the *perhaps*" (Derrida, *Specters*, 42; emphasis in the original). See also Dickens's four "Supposing" articles from *Household Words*.

EPILOGUE

1. For useful discussions of the story that also note its emphasis on personal loss, see Parker, *Christmas and Charles Dickens*, 275–79, and Slater, 338.

2. Dickens, "What Christmas Is," 21. Subsequent page references will be noted parenthetically in the text.

3. Dickens, *Great Expectations*, 173. On this figure, see Jordan, "Partings Welded Together."

4. Dickens's sister Fanny had died in September 1848. Her death was followed only a few months later by that of her crippled son. See Slater, *Charles Dickens*, 279, 338.

5. For a reading of *A Christmas Carol* and Joyce's "The Dead" along these lines, one that I find congenial, see Saint-Amour, "'Christmas Yet to Come.'"

APPENDIX

1. Steig, *Dickens and Phiz*, 18.

2. For a description of this process, see Harvey, *Victorian Novelists and Their Illustrators*, 183.

3. Steig, *Dickens and Phiz*, 156; Cohen, *Dickens and His Original Illustrators*, 112; Lester, *Phiz*, 155.

4. Steig, *Dickens and Phiz*, 18.

5. In anticipation of the wear to which his steels would be subjected by repeated strikings, Browne made duplicates of the ten dark plates for *Bleak House*, including "The Mausoleum at Chesney Wold." Slight differences exist between the two versions. So far as I am able to determine, however, the differences do not affect the area immediately in front of the mausoleum door. For guidance in distinguishing the two versions, see Johannsen, *Phiz Illustrations*, 412–13.

Johannsen identifies the two versions as "Plate A" and "Plate B." My figure 9 is a Plate A. The Penguin edition illustration is a Plate B. The reproductions in Johannsen are not of high enough resolution to be helpful in settling the question of whether there is a figure standing before the mausoleum door.

6. Quoted in Lester, *Phiz*, 154.

7. Johannsen states that the novel's dark plates "apparently were all printed directly from the steels, while the remaining 30 plates were both lithographed and printed from the steels" (*Phiz Illustrations*, 397). In most of the copies I have examined, the mausoleum plate appears to be an etching, but the possibility that some dark plates were lithographed still remains.

8. Illustrations for the Nonesuch edition were made directly from Browne's original steel plates.

9. Dickens, *Oliver Twist*, 368.

BIBLIOGRAPHY

Abraham, Nicolas, and Maria Torok. *The Shell and the Kernel: Renewals of Psychoanalysis.* Trans. and ed. Nicholas T. Rand. Chicago: University of Chicago Press, 1994.
Arac, Jonathan. *Commissioned Spirits: The Shaping of Social Motion in Dickens, Carlyle, Melville, and Hawthorne.* New Brunswick, NJ: Rutgers University Press, 1979.
Bal, Mieke. *Narratology: Introduction to the Theory of Narrative.* 2nd ed. Toronto: University of Toronto Press, 1997.
———. *Reading "Rembrandt": Beyond the Word-Image Opposition.* Cambridge: Cambridge University Press, 1991.
Barthes, Roland. "The Grain of the Voice." In *Image-Music-Text,* trans. Stephen Heath, 179–89. New York: Hill and Wang, 1977.
Bigelow, Gordon. *Fiction, Famine, and the Rise of Economics in Victorian Britain and Ireland.* Cambridge: Cambridge University Press, 2003.
Birch, Dennis. "A Forgotten Book: Extracts from a Talk on *A Child's History of England* Given to the Dickens Fellowship of London." *Dickensian* 51 (1955): 121–26; 154–57.
Bodenheimer, Rosemarie. *Knowing Dickens.* Ithaca, NY: Cornell University Press, 2007.
Bollas, Christopher. *The Shadow of the Object: Psychoanalysis of the Unthought Known.* New York: Columbia University Press, 1987.
Brau, Jean-Louis, ed. *La voix narrative.* Nice: Publication de la Faculté des Lettres, Arts et Sciences Humaines, 2001.
Brooks, Peter. *Reading for the Plot: Design and Intention in Narrative.* New York: Knopf, 1984.

Bryson, Norman. "Introduction: Art and Intersubjectivity." In *Looking In: The Art of Viewing*, 139–45. Amsterdam: G+B Arts International, 2001.

Budd, Dona. "Language Couples in *Bleak House*." *Nineteenth-Century Literature* 49 (1994): 196–220.

Buzard, James. *Disorienting Fiction: The Autoethnographic Work of Nineteenth-Century British Novelists*. Princeton, NJ: Princeton University Press, 2005.

Carlisle, Janice. "The Crystal Palace and Dickens's 'Dark Exhibition.'" In *Approaches to Teaching Dickens's "Bleak House,"* ed. John O. Jordan and Gordon Bigelow, 31–37. New York: Modern Language Association, 2008.

Carlyle, Thomas. *The French Revolution: A History*. Ed. K. J. Fielding and David Sorenson. Oxford: Oxford University Press, 1989.

———. *Past and Present*. Ed. Richard D. Altick. New York: New York University Press, 1977.

Caruth, Cathy. *Unclaimed Experience: Trauma, Narrative, and History*. Baltimore: Johns Hopkins University Press, 1996.

Case, Alison. "Gender and History in Narrative Theory: The Problem of Retrospective Distance in *David Copperfield* and *Bleak House*." In *A Companion to Narrative Theory*, ed. James Phelan and Peter J. Rabinowitz, 312–21. Malden, MA: Blackwell, 2005.

Cohen, Jane R. *Charles Dickens and His Original Illustrators*. Columbus: Ohio State University Press, 1980.

Collins, Philip. *Dickens and Education*. London: Macmillan, 1963.

Connor, Steven. *Dumbstruck: A Cultural History of Ventriloquism*. Oxford: Oxford University Press, 2000.

Culler, Jonathan. "Story and Discourse in the Analysis of Narrative." In *The Pursuit of Signs: Semiotics, Literature, Deconstruction*, 169–87. Ithaca, NY: Cornell University Press, 1981.

Cummings, Katherine. *Telling Tales: The Hysteric's Seduction in Fiction and Theory*. Stanford, CA: Stanford University Press, 1991.

Daleski, H. M. *Dickens and the Art of Analogy*. New York: Schocken, 1970.

Derrida, Jacques. "Le Facteur de la verité." *Poétique* 6 (1975): 96–147.

———. *Specters of Marx: The State of the Debt, the Work of Mourning, and the New International*. Trans. Peggy Kamuf. New York: Routledge, 1994.

Dever, Carolyn. *Death and the Mother from Dickens to Freud: Victorian Fiction and the Anxiety of Origins*. Cambridge: Cambridge University Press, 1998.

Dickens, Charles. *Bleak House*. London: Bradbury and Evans, 1852–53.

———. *Bleak House*. London: Nonesuch, 1938. Facsimile edition. London: Duckworth, 2005.

———. *Bleak House: An Authoritative and Annotated Text*. Ed. George Ford and Sylvère Monod. Norton Critical Edition. New York: Norton, 1977.

———. *Bleak House*. Harmondsworth: Penguin, 2003.

———. *David Copperfield*. Ed. Nina Burgis. Oxford: Clarendon Press, 1981.

———. *Dombey and Son.* Ed. Alan Horsman. Oxford: Clarendon Press, 1974.
———. *Great Expectations: Authoritative Text, Backgrounds, Contexts, Criticism.* Ed. Edgar Rosenberg. Norton Critical Edition. New York: Norton, 1999.
———. *The Letters of Charles Dickens.* Ed. Madeline House, Graham Storey, and Kathleen Tillotson. Pilgrim Edition. 12 vols. Oxford: Clarendon Press, 1965–2002.
———. *"Master Humphrey's Clock" and "A Child's History of England."* Oxford: Oxford University Press, 1958.
———. *Oliver Twist.* Ed. Kathleen Tillotson. Oxford: Clarendon Press, 1966.
———. *The Speeches of Charles Dickens.* Ed. K. J. Fielding. Atlantic Highlands, NJ: Humanities Press International, 1988.
———. "What Christmas Is As We Grow Older." In *Christmas Stories,* 19–25. London: Oxford University Press, 1959.
[Dickens, Charles]. "Supposing!" *Household Words* 1 (April 20, 1850): 96.
———. "Supposing." *Household Words* 1 (August 10, 1850): 480.
———. "Supposing." *Household Words* 3 (June 7, 1851): 264.
———. "Supposing." *Household Words* 3 (September 6, 1851): 576.
Dickens, Mamie. "Charles Dickens at Home, by His Eldest Daughter." *Cornhill Magazine* n.s. 4 (1885): 32–51.
———. *My Father As I Knew Him.* London: Roxburghe Press, 1896.
Eigner, Edwin. *The Metaphysical Novel in England and America: Dickens, Bulwer, Melville, and Hawthorne.* Berkeley and Los Angeles: University of California Press, 1978.
Fielding, K. J., and Alec W. Brice. "*Bleak House* and the Graveyard." In *Dickens the Craftsman,* ed. Robert J. Partlow Jr., 115–39. Carbondale: Southern Illinois University Press, 1970.
Fletcher, John, ed. *Essays on Otherness.* London: Routledge, 1999.
Fletcher, LuAnn McCracken. "A Recipe for Perversion: The Feminine Narrative Challenge in *Bleak House.*" *Dickens Studies Annual: Essays in Victorian Fiction* 25 (1996): 67–89.
Forster, John. *The Life of Charles Dickens.* 2 vols. New York: Baker and Taylor, 1911.
Frank, Lawrence. *Charles Dickens and the Romantic Self.* Lincoln: University of Nebraska Press, 1984.
Freud, Sigmund. *Beyond the Pleasure Principle.* Trans. James Strachey. New York: Norton, 1989.
———. "From the History of an Infantile Neurosis." In *Three Case Histories,* ed. Philip Rieff, 187–316. New York: Collier, 1963.
———. "Mourning and Melancholia." In *Collected Papers,* trans. and ed. Joan Riviere, 4: 152–70. New York: Basic Books, 1959.
———. *The Uncanny.* Trans. David McLintock. London: Penguin, 2003.

Friedman, Stanley. "A Considerate Ghost: George Rouncewell in *Bleak House*." *Dickens Studies Annual: Essays on Victorian Fiction* 17 (1988): 111–28.

———. *Dickens's Fiction: Tapestries of Conscience*. New York: AMS Press, 2003.

Gardiner, John. "Dickens and the Uses of History." In *A Companion to Charles Dickens*, ed. David Paroissien, 240–54. Malden, MA: Blackwell, 2008.

Genette, Gérard. *Narrative Discourse: An Essay in Method*. Trans. Jane E. Lewin. Ithaca, NY: Cornell University Press, 1980.

Gilbert, Elliot, ed. *Critical Essays on Charles Dickens's "Bleak House."* Boston: Hall, 1979.

Glavin, John. *After Dickens: Reading, Adaptation, and Performance*. Cambridge: Cambridge University Press, 1999.

Goodman, Marcia Renee. "'I'll follow the other': Tracing the (M)Other in *Bleak House*." *Dickens Studies Annual: Essays on Victorian Fiction* 19 (1990): 147–67.

Gottfried, Barbara. "Fathers and Suitors: Narratives of Desire in *Bleak House*." *Dickens Studies Annual: Essays on Victorian Fiction* 19 (1990): 169–203.

———. "Household Arrangements and the Patriarchal Order in *Bleak House*." *Journal of Narrative Technique* 24 (1994): 1–17.

Graver, Suzanne. "Writing in a 'Womanly' Way and the Double Vision of *Bleak House*." *Dickens Quarterly* 4 (1987): 3–15.

Green, André. "The Dead Mother." In *On Private Madness*, 142–73. Madison, CT: International Universities Press, 1986.

Hack, Daniel. *The Material Interests of the Victorian Novel*. Charlottesville: University of Virginia Press, 2005.

Harvey, John R. *Victorian Novelists and Their Illustrators*. New York: New York University Press, 1971.

Hatton, Thomas, and Arthur J. Cleaver. *A Bibliography of the Periodical Works of Charles Dickens: Bibliographical, Analytical, and Statistical*. London: Chapman and Hall, 1933.

Herbert, Christopher. "The Occult in *Bleak House*." *Novel: A Forum on Fiction* 17 (1984): 101–15.

Hochman, Baruch, and Ilja Wachs. *Dickens: The Orphan Condition*. Madison, NJ: Fairleigh Dickinson University Press, 1999.

Hutter, Albert D. "The High Tower of His Mind: Psychoanalysis and the Reader of *Bleak House*." *Criticism: A Quarterly for Literature and the Arts* 19 (1977): 296–316.

Jaffe, Audrey. *Vanishing Points: Dickens, Narrative, and the Subject of Omniscience*. Berkeley and Los Angeles: University of California Press, 1991.

Jann, Rosemary. "Fact, Fiction, and Interpretation in *A Child's History of England*." *Dickens Quarterly* 4 (1987): 199–205.

Johannsen, Albert. *Phiz Illustrations from the Novels of Charles Dickens*. Chicago: University of Chicago Press, 1956.

Jordan, John O., ed. *The Cambridge Companion to Charles Dickens.* Cambridge: Cambridge University Press, 2001.

———. "Partings Welded Together: Self-Fashioning in *Great Expectations* and *Jane Eyre.*" *Dickens Quarterly* 13 (1996): 19–33.

———. "The Social Sub-text of *David Copperfield.*" *Dickens Studies Annual: Essays on Victorian Fiction* 14 (1985): 61–92.

Jordan, John O., and Gordon Bigelow, ed. *Approaches to Teaching Dickens's "Bleak House."* New York: Modern Language Association, 2008.

Kaplan, Fred. *Dickens and Mesmerism: The Hidden Springs of Fiction.* Princeton, NJ: Princeton University Press, 1975.

Lacan, Jacques. "Seminar on 'The Purloined Letter.'" Trans. Jeffrey Mehlman. In *The Purloined Poe: Lacan, Derrida, and Psychoanalytic Reading,* ed. John P. Muller and William J. Richardson, 28–54. Baltimore: Johns Hopkins University Press, 1988.

Lai, Shu-Fang. "*Bleak House* and Victorian Science." In *Approaches to Teaching Dickens's "Bleak House,"* ed. John O. Jordan and Gordon Bigelow, 64–70. New York: Modern Language Association, 2008.

Laplanche, Jacques. "Notes on Afterwardsness." In *Essays on Otherness,* ed. John Fletcher, 260–65. London: Routledge, 1999.

Ledger, Sally. *Dickens and the Popular Radical Imagination.* Cambridge: Cambridge University Press, 2007.

Leicester, H. Marshall, Jr. *The Disenchanted Self: Representing the Subject in the "Canterbury Tales."* Berkeley and Los Angeles: University of California Press, 1990.

Leonardi, Susan J., and Rebecca A. Pope. *The Diva's Mouth: Body, Voice, Prima Donna Politics.* New Brunswick, NJ: Rutgers University Press, 1996.

Lester, Valerie. *Phiz: The Man Who Drew Dickens.* London: Chatto and Windus, 2004.

Levinas, Emmanuel. *Time and the Other.* Trans. Richard A. Cohen. Pittsburgh: Duquesne University Press, 1987.

Lohrli, Anne. *"Household Words": A Weekly Journal, 1850–1859, Conducted by Charles Dickens. Table of Contents, List of Contributors and Their Contributions Based on the "Household Words" Office Book.* Toronto: University of Toronto Press, 1973.

Lucas, John. "Past and Present: *Bleak House* and *A Child's History of England.*" In *Dickens Refigured: Desires, Bodies and Other Histories,* ed. John Schad, 136–56. Manchester: Manchester University Press, 1996.

Lukacher, Ned. *Primal Scenes: Literature, Philosophy, Psychoanalysis.* Ithaca, NY: Cornell University Press, 1986.

Maxwell, Richard, ed. *The Victorian Illustrated Book.* Charlottesville: University of Virginia Press, 2002.

McLaughlin, Kevin. *Paperwork: Fiction and Mass Mediacy in the Paper Age.* Philadelphia: University of Pennsylvania Press, 2005.

Michie, Helena. "'Who is this in pain?': Scarring, Disfigurement, and Identity in *Bleak House* and *Our Mutual Friend*." *Novel: A Forum on Fiction* 22 (1989): 199–212.

Miller, Andrew. *Novels behind Glass: Commodity Culture and Victorian Narrative*. Cambridge: Cambridge University Press, 1995.

Miller, D. A. *The Novel and the Police*. Berkeley and Los Angeles: University of California Press, 1988.

Miller, J. Hillis. *Charles Dickens: The World of His Novels*. Cambridge, MA: Harvard University Press, 1958.

———. Introduction to *Bleak House*. Harmondsworth: Penguin, 1971.

Muller, John P., and William J. Richardson, eds. *The Purloined Poe: Lacan, Derrida, and Psychoanalytic Reading*. Baltimore: Johns Hopkins University Press, 1988.

Newsom, Robert. *Dickens on the Romantic Side of Familiar Things: "Bleak House" and the Novel Tradition*. New York: Columbia University Press, 1977.

Parker, David. *Christmas and Charles Dickens*. New York: AMS Press, 2005.

Paroissien, David, ed. *A Companion to Charles Dickens*. Malden, MA: Blackwell, 2008.

Partlow, Robert, Jr., ed. *Dickens the Craftsman*. Carbondale: Southern Illinois University Press, 1970.

Patten, Robert L. "Plot and the Plot of *Bleak House*." In *Approaches to Teaching Dickens's "Bleak House,"* ed. John O. Jordan and Gordon Bigelow, 92–98. New York: Modern Language Association, 2008.

———. "Serial Illustration and Storytelling in *David Copperfield*." In *The Victorian Illustrated Book*, ed. Richard Maxwell, 91–128. Charlottesville: University of Virginia Press, 2002.

Peltason, Timothy. "The Esther Problem." In *Approaches to Teaching Dickens's "Bleak House,"* ed. John O. Jordan and Gordon Bigelow, 71–78. New York: Modern Language Association, 2008.

———. "Esther's Will." *ELH* 59 (1992): 671–91.

Phelan, James, and Peter J. Rabinowitz, ed. *A Companion to Narrative Theory*. Malden, MA: Blackwell, 2005.

Ragussis, Michael. "The Ghostly Signs of *Bleak House*." *Nineteenth-Century Fiction* 34 (1979): 253–80.

Sadrin, Anny. "Charlotte Dickens: The Female Narrator of *Bleak House*." *Dickens Quarterly* 9 (1992): 47–57.

Saint-Amour, Paul. "'Christmas Yet to Come': Hospitality, Futurity, the *Carol*, and 'The Dead.'" *Representations* 98 (2007): 93–117.

Schad, John, ed. *Dickens Refigured: Desires, Bodies and Other Histories*. Manchester: Manchester University Press, 1996.

Schor, Hilary. *Dickens and the Daughter of the House*. Cambridge: Cambridge University Press, 1999.

Shatto, Susan. *The Companion to "Bleak House."* Boston: Unwin Hyman, 1988.

Sicher, Ephraim. *Rereading the City/Rereading Dickens: Representation, the Novel, and Urban Realism.* New York: AMS Press, 2003.

Siegel, Daniel J. *The Developing Mind: How Relationships and the Brain Interact to Shape Who We Are.* New York: Guilford, 1999.

Slater, Michael. *Charles Dickens.* New Haven, CT: Yale University Press, 2009.

Steig, Michael. *Dickens and Phiz.* Bloomington: Indiana University Press, 1978.

Stein, Richard L. "*Bleak House* and Illustration: Learning to Look." In *Approaches to Teaching Dickens's "Bleak House,"* ed. John O. Jordan and Gordon Bigelow, 106–112. New York: Modern Language Association, 2008.

——. "Dickens and Illustration." In *The Cambridge Companion to Charles Dickens,* ed. John O. Jordan, 167–88. Cambridge: Cambridge University Press, 2001.

Sternlieb, Lisa. *The Female Narrator in the British Novel: Hidden Agendas.* New York: Palgrave, 2002.

——. "What Esther Knew." In *Approaches to Teaching Dickens's "Bleak House,"* ed. John O. Jordan and Gordon Bigelow, 79–84. New York: Modern Language Association, 2008.

Stewart, Garrett. "The New Mortality of *Bleak House.*" *ELH* 45 (1978): 443–87.

Stolorow, Robert D., and George E. Atwood. *Contexts of Being: The Intersubjective Foundations of Psychological Life.* Hillsdale, NJ: Analytic Press, 1992.

Sucksmith, Harvey Peter. "Sir Leicester Dedlock, Wat Tyler, and the Chartists: The Role of the Ironmaster in *Bleak House.*" *Dickens Studies Annual: Essays on Victorian Fiction* 4 (1975): 113–31.

Thackeray, William Makepeace. *Vanity Fair: A Novel without A Hero.* London: Bradbury and Evans, 1848.

Torgovnick, Marianna. *Closure in the Novel.* Princeton, NJ: Princeton University Press, 1981.

Tracy, Robert. "Lighthousekeeping: *Bleak House* and the Crystal Palace." *Dickens Studies Annual: Essays on Victorian Fiction* 33 (2003): 25–53.

Vanden Bossche, Chris R. "Class Discourse and Popular Agency in *Bleak House.*" *Victorian Studies* 47 (2004): 7–31.

Welsh, Alexander. *Dickens Redressed: The Art of "Bleak House" and "Hard Times."* New Haven, CT: Yale University Press, 2000.

West, Gilian. "*Bleak House:* Esther's Illness." *English Studies: A Journal of English Language and Literature* 73 (1992): 30–34.

Wilkinson, Ann Y. "*Bleak House:* From Faraday to Judgment Day." *ELH* 34 (1967): 225–47.

Williams, Raymond. *Marxism and Literature.* Oxford: Oxford University Press, 1977.

Wilt, Judith. "Confusion and Consciousness in Dickens's Esther." *Nineteenth-Century Fiction* 32 (1977): 285–309.

Winnicott, D. W. "Transitional Objects and Transitional Phenomena." In *Playing and Reality,* 1–25. New York: Routledge, 1971.

INDEX

Italicized page numbers refer to illustrations.

Abraham, Nicolas, 75, 165n4, 167n10
absence and presence, theme of, 143
Ada, 15–17, 35, 54–56, 57
Alfred the Great (king), 123–24
"appointed time, The," illustration, 28, *29*, 136
"attraction of repulsion," 7, 106

Bal, Mieke, 27, 42, 82
"Becky's second appearance in the character of Clytemnestra" illustration, 150, *151*
Benveniste, Émile, 27
betrayal, 3, 48, 56–57, 111. *See also* faithfulness
Beyond the Pleasure Principle (Freud), 44, 64
Bigelow, Gordon, 2
biphasic model of trauma, 45–46, 47. *See also* trauma
"blank depression," 24–25, 49, 52–54, 57, 61, 110. *See also* depression
Bleak House (Dickens): autobiographical elements in, 92–97, 98, 107–12; beginning of writing, 88, 111; Dora Dickens in, 108–12; endings in, 68, 71–73, 76–83, 85–86; first idea for, 88, 102, 105–6; ghosts in, 6, 82, 111, 114–20, 134–37; as a ghost story, 102, 114; "great turning idea" of, 163n23; as historical novel, 122–23, 129, 131–40; illustrations in first edition, 154–57; infant deaths in, 15–17, 109–10, 119; John Dickens in, 107–8; narrators as ghosts, 137; parallels with Dickens's life, 107–12; parallels with *Oliver Twist*, 108; as social novel, 113; and "What Christmas Is," 142
Boadicea (queen), 125, 132
Bodenheimer, Rosemarie, 89, 92, 98–99
Bollas, Christopher, 22
Bradbury and Evans (publishers), 82, 155–56
Breuer, Josef, 44
Brooks, Peter, 4, 5
Browne, Hablot K. ("Phiz"): as *Bleak House* illustrator, 26–27, 168n5 (Appendix); Elkins drawing, 152–53, *153*; first edition lithography, *157*;

Browne, Hablot K. ("Phiz") (*continued*)
Gimbel drawing, 153–54, *155;* letter from Dickens, 150–52; on lithography, 82, 156; Nonesuch edition, *158. See also* illustrations

Bucket, Inspector: as avatar of Dickens, 95–96; as Orpheus, 60–63; as psychoanalyst, 61–65, 74, 95–96; speech mannerisms and gestures, 63–65

Buzard, James, 2

Carlyle, Thomas, 132, 133
Caruth, Cathy, 46–47, 121–22
charity, genuine, 138
Charles I (king), 126–27
Charles II (king), 128
Chesney Wold: ghost of, 122; as haunted house, 117–18; as synecdoche for the nation, 85
childhood, Dickens's interest in, 88–89
Child's History of England, A (Dickens), 123–29, 167n11; as allegory, 128–29; narrative shape of, 126–27; women leaders in, 125–26
Christmas, 141–45
Christmas Carol, A (Dickens), 130
"Christmas Tree, A" (Dickens), 141
class structure, 57, 133
Cleaver, Arthur, 160
"Close of Esther's Narrative, The," chapter, 75–79
Cohen, Jane R., 152
Collins, Philip, 123
common decency, acts of, 57
Communist Manifesto (Marx), 129
Companion to "Bleak House" (Shatto), 166n5 (chap. 5)
confusion, rhetoric of, 10, 161n6
"Consecrated ground" illustration, 31–34, *34,* 163n4
Cromwell, Elizabeth, as Dora Dickens, 128
Cromwell, Oliver, 127–28

cross-generational transmission of trauma, 45, 167n10. *See also* trauma
Cruikshank, George, 159, *159*

dark plates: print quality of, 82, 156, 168n5 (Appendix), 169n7; retrospective focalization of, 37; use with dual narrators, 27. *See also* "Ghost's Walk, The"; "Mausoleum at Chesney Wold, The"; "Sunset in the long Drawing-room at Chesney Wold"

David Copperfield (Dickens): as autobiographical novel, 88; Charles I in, 126–27; Dora Spenlow Copperfield in, 99, 100–101, 108–9, 118; finished writing, 102; ghosts from Dickens's past in, 118–19; illustrations in, 91; infant memory in, 89–91; interpretation of, 94–95; John Dickens in, 107

"Dead Mother, The" (Green), 48, 109
dead mother complex, 48–50
Death and the Mother from Dickens to Freud (Dever), 2–3
deaths, infant, 15, 17, 109–10, 119
Dedlock family as history of England, 120–21
"deferred action" (*Nachträglichkeit*), 45, 47
depression, 48–49, 50, 52, 101, 109. *See also* "blank depression"
Derrida, Jacques, 129–31, 136, 138–39, 165n5, 168n25
Dever, Carolyn, 2–3, 7, 15, 16, 27, 54–55
Dickens, Catherine (Kate), 99–100; becoming ill, 101–2; and death of Dora, 104–5; as Esther, 110; as Lady Dedlock, 109, 110; nervous depression, 101, 109
Dickens, Charles: autobiographical fragment, 88, 93–94, 107; beginning to write *Bleak House,* 88, 111; biographical parallels with *Bleak House,* 107–12; birth of daughter

INDEX

Dora, 99–101; and Christmas, 141–45; control of narrative form, 126–27; death of Dora Annie, 103–6; English Civil War and, 167n15; first idea for *Bleak House*, 88, 102, 105–6; "great turning idea" of *Bleak House*, 163n23; interest in childhood, 88–89; mirrors and, 91–92, 165n3 (chap. 5); naming practices, 11; self-references in characters, 92–97; use of writing conventions, 76, 128; writing as a ghost, 112

Dickens, Dora Annie: as biographical ghost, 111, 119; birth of, 99–101; death of, 103–6; in "What Christmas Is," 144

Dickens, John, 103, 107–8

Dickens, Mary (Mamie), 91–92, 104

Dickens Project (University of California), 2, 161n1

discourse, free indirect, 34, 42, 50

disfigurement of Esther, 18, 24–25, 53–54

dolls: Esther and, 11–12, 14, 40, 52, 56; in "The appointed time" illustration, 28, 136

Dombey and Son (Dickens), 59–60, 88

"Down in Lincolnshire" chapter, 79–80, 85

Elliotson, John, 89

"emancipatory promise," 131, 138. *See also* justice

England, history of, as story of trauma, 120–22

English Civil War, 120, 167n15

énoncé, 70. *See also sjužet* and *fabula*

enunciation, 4, 70

Esther: as comic vocalist, 15; critical views on voice of, 73; dead mother complex, 52; death of brickmaker's baby, 15–17; departure from Windsor, 12–13; discovery of mother's body, 1–2, 68–71; disfigurement of, 18, 24–25, 53–54;

and dolls, 11–12, 14, 40, 52, 56; as Eurydice, 60–63; false identities of, 11; figurative language, 22; as ghost, 6, 84–85, 118; ghostly encounters, 22–24; as "Good Esther," 9–10, 27, 52, 78, 84; internal focalization of illustrations, 34; Lady Dedlock encounter in church, 17–21; letters from Lady Dedlock, 6, 7–9, 47–48, 54–55, 65, 68; marriage to Woodcourt, 71–72; mirrors and, 14, 52–54, 57, 92, 164n8 (chap. 3); and mother's rejection, 3, 15, 19; as mother to others, 10; mysterious illness, 21, 24; as narrator, 2, 3, 4–6, 7, 11–12, 14, 15, 77, 161n6; "psychoanalysis" of, 71, 72–73, 74, 78; resemblance to Dora Dickens, 109; as retreating to background, 11–12; reunion with Ada, 54–56, 57; reunion with mother, 54–56; rhetoric of confusion and, 10, 161n6; self-abasement, 12; self-awareness of, 7, 8; significance of names, 3, 11; and story of her birth, 6–7, 8; and Victorian values, 9

Eurydice-Orpheus analogy, 60–65, 74

external focalization, 42, 84

fabula and *sjužet*, 4, 24, 35, 70

faithfulness, 56–57. *See also* betrayal

false identities, 11

false voice, 9–10

farewell scenes, 14

figurative language, 13, 22

Fitz-Osbert, William (Longbeard), 124

focalization: character-based, 31; concept of, 27, 118, 163n1; external, 42, 84; heteroperceptive, 28, 42, 82, 118; homoperceptive, 35, 42, 118; internal, 28, 82, 84; retrospective, 35–36, 38, 41, 84, 91; shift in, 8–9

Fort/Da game, 64

Frank, Lawrence, 2, 164n8 (chap. 3)

free indirect discourse, 34, 42, 50

free indirect perception, 42, 82, 84, 118
French Revolution, The (Carlyle), 132
Freud, Sigmund, 44–45, 47, 51, 64
Friedman, Stanley, 108

gender stereotypes, 122
Genette, Gérard, 27, 28, 162n15
George, Mr., 56, 110, 132–34
ghosts: in *Bleak House,* 114–16, 119–20; of Chesney Wold, 85; from Dickens's past, 118–19; Dora Dickens as biographical, 119; encounters with, 22–24; Esther and her mother as, 6, 118; haunted houses, 117–18; historical, 131, 137–39; in illustrations, 82–84; narrators of *Bleak House* as, 137; in *Oliver Twist,* 157–60; of ordinary people, 134–37; in "The Mausoleum at Chesney Wold," 148–49; in "What Christmas Is," 144
ghost story: *Bleak House* as, 114; *A Child's History of England* as, 129; historical, 121–22
Ghost's Walk, 13
"Ghost's Walk, The," illustration, 37, *37*
ghostwriting, 38, 74, 84, 111, 118
gift, concept of, 130–31, 138
Glavin, John, 2
"Good Esther," 9–10, 27, 52, 78, 84
Goodman, Marcia, 2
Gottfried, Barbara, 2
Great Expectations (Dickens), 143
Green, André, 48–50, 52, 54, 109
Guppy, 29–30, 53, 83, 98, 115, 148
Guster, 137–38

Hades/Pluto analogy, 58–60
Hamlet, 130–31
Hampden, John, 127, 167n15
Hatton, Thomas, 160
haunted houses, 117–18. *See also* ghosts
"Haunted Man, The" (Dickens), 89
Hawdon, Captain. *See* Nemo
Heidegger, Martin, 131, 138–39

heterodiegetic narrator, concept of, 28
heteroperceptive focalization, 28, 42, 82, 118
homoperceptive focalization, 35, 42, 118
Hortense, 18, 20–21, 31, 132
Household Words (Dickens), 88, 141
Hutter, Albert D., 2

illustrations, 79–83; in *Bleak House,* 26–43; first edition, 154–57; ghosts in, 82–83; graphic styles of, 27; list of illustrations, viii; verbal text vs., 149–50. *See also* Browne, Hablot K. ("Phiz"); dark plates; focalization; *specific illustrations*
infant deaths, 15–17, 109–10, 119. *See also* Dickens, Dora Annie
infant memory, 89–91
ink, 82–84, 97
internal focalization, 28, 82, 84
intra-Dickensian intertextuality, 108
Ironmaster (Mr. Rouncewell), 132–34

Jaffe, Audrey, 2
James II (king), 128
Jo, 31–33, 84, 137–39
Joan of Arc, 125–26, 132
Johannsen, Albert, 168n5 (Appendix), 169n7
justice, 129–32, 137–39, 145

Kaplan, Fred, 2, 95–96
Knowing Dickens (Bodenheimer), 89

Lady Dedlock: Catherine Dickens as, 109, 110; death of, 1–2, 14, 66; as emotionally dead, 50–51; encounter with Esther in church, 17–21; as ghost, 6, 118; letters from, 6, 7–9, 47–48, 54–55, 65, 68; as Proserpine/Persephone, 58–60; renouncing secrecy, 67–68
"Lady Dedlock in the Wood" illustration, 37–42, *39*
Ledger, Sally, 2

INDEX

Lester, Valerie Browne, 152
Levinas, Emmanuel, 139
lithography, 82, 155–56. *See also* illustrations
"little church in the park, The," illustration, 30–31, 32–33, 35
"Little old Lady, The," illustration, 35–36, *36*, 164n5 (chap. 2)
Lucas, John, 129

"Magnanimous conduct of Mr. Guppy" illustration, 80
marriage, 71–72, 128
Marx, Karl, 129
"Mausoleum at Chesney Wold, The," illustration, 80–83, *81*, 150; Elkins drawing, 152–53, *153*; first edition lithography, *157*; ghost in, 148–49; Gimbel drawing, 153–54, *155*; Nonesuch edition, *158*
memory, 5–6; fragments of, 15; theme of, 89–91
mesmerism, 95–96
Michie, Helena, 2
Miller, D. A., 113–14
Miller, J. Hillis, 96
"mirror-identification," 49–50
mirrors, Dickens and, 91–92, 165n3
mirror scenes, 36, 52–54, 164n8 (chap. 3)
"Mr. Guppy's desolation" illustration, 29–30, *30*, 35
mother's rejection, 3, 15, 19
mythic structure, 57–63; Eurydice-Orpheus analogy, 60–63; Proserpine-Pluto analogy, 58–60

Nachträglichkeit ("deferred action"), 45, 47
naming practices, 11
narration/narrators: difficulty in distinguishing, 161n6; free indirect discourse, 34, 42, 50; structure of repetition in, 4; unnamed present-tense, 28, 87, 112, 137; voice in, 3, 11–12, 162n15. *See also* Esther; focalization
Nemo (Captain Hawdon): as ghost of common people, 134–35; and ink, 83; and Lady Dedlock's depression, 50; significance of iron gate imagery, 14, 162n18; as unseen viewer in "Consecrated ground" illustration, 31–34
Newsom, Robert, 2, 107, 147

Oliver Twist (Dickens), 88; ghosts in, 157–60; infant memory in, 89–91; parallels with *Bleak House*, 108; "Rose Maylie and Oliver" illustration in, *159*
Orpheus-Eurydice analogy, 60–63

Past and Present (Carlyle), 133
Patten, Robert, 2, 163n1
perception, free indirect, 42, 82, 84, 118
post-traumatic stress disorder (PTSD), 45
presence and absence, theme of, 143
primal scenes, 6, 15, 41, 45, 47–48, 69
Proserpine/Persephone analogy, 58–60
prosopopoeia, trope of, 8
psychoanalysis, 3, 44–66; Inspector Bucket and, 61–65, 74, 95–96. *See also* dead mother complex; trauma

Rachael, Mrs., 13–14
"reactive symmetry," 54
remarques, 152
Reprinted Pieces (Dickens), 88
retrospective focalization, 35–36, 38, 41, 84; of illustrations in *David Copperfield*, 91
"Rose Maylie and Oliver" illustration, *159*
Rouncewell, George (Mr. George), 56, 110, 132–34
Rouncewell, Mr. (Ironmaster), 132–34

Rouncewell, Mrs., as Dickens's grandmother, 166n5 (chap. 5)
Rouncewell, Watt, as James Watt, 131–32

Schor, Hilary, 2, 114
seduction theory, 44. *See also* trauma
self-abasement of Esther, 10
self-references, meta-fictional, 97–98
"shadowy world," 102
Shatto, Susan, 166n5 (chap. 5)
Shell and the Kernel (Abraham and Torok), 165n4
"Sir Leicester Dedlock" illustration, 40–41
sjužet and *fabula*, 4, 24, 35, 70
Skimpole, 92, 93–94, 107–8
Snagsby, Mrs., as a ghost, 114
social novel, *Bleak House* as, 113
specters. *See* ghosts
Specters of Marx (Derrida), 129
Steig, Michael, 152, 154
Stein, Richard L., 2
Stewart, Garrett, 2
Stolorow, Robert, 45–46, 47
subject positions, confusion of, 3–4
summaries, convention of, 76
Summerson, Esther. *See* Esther
"Sunset in the long Drawing-room at Chesney Wold" illustration, 116–17, 117–18
"supposing," 78–79, 165nn5–6

temporality: double, 34–35, 38, 40; in narrative, 3, 5, 7, 8
Thackeray, William Makepeace, 150, *151*
"Tom," 135–36
"Tom-all-Alone's" illustration, 136

Torok, Maria, 75, 165n4, 167n10
Tracy, Robert, 2
trauma: biphasic model of, 45–46, 47; cross-generational transmission of, 45, 167n7; history of England as story of, 121–22; of maternal loss, 9; repeated, 144; studies, 44–48. *See also* psychoanalysis
Tulkinghorn as Hades/Pluto, 58–60
Tyler, Wat, 125, 131–32

"Uncanny, The" (Freud), 45
Unclaimed Experience: Trauma, Narrative, and History (Caruth), 46–47, 121–22
"unknown friend," 17, 75, 97
"unthought known," 22–24, 41

Vanden Bossche, Chris R., 114
Vanity Fair: A Novel without a Hero (Thackeray), 150, *151*
verbal text, privilege of, 149–50
Victoria (queen), 128, 137
Victorian values, 9
voice in narrative, 3, 11–12, 162n15
voice-oriented reading, 12–15, 17
Volumnia, 85–86

watching, inanimate, 28–29
Welsh, Alexander, 107, 161n6
"What Christmas Is As We Grow Older" (Dickens), 141–45
Williams, Raymond, 133
Wolf Man case study (Freud), 44, 45
Woodcourt, Esther. *See* Esther

"Young Man of the name of Guppy, The," illustration, 51, *51*

Recent Books in the Victorian Literature
and Culture Series

Barbara J. Black
On Exhibit: Victorians and Their Museums

Annette R. Federico
Idol of Suburbia: Marie Corelli and Late-Victorian Literary Culture

Talia Schaffer
The Forgotten Female Aesthetes: Literary Culture in Late-Victorian England

Julia F. Saville
A Queer Chivalry: The Homoerotic Asceticism of Gerard Manley Hopkins

Victor Shea and William Whitla, Editors
Essays and Reviews: The 1860 Text and Its Reading

Marlene Tromp
The Private Rod: Marital Violence, Sensation, and the Law in Victorian Britain

Dorice Williams Elliott
The Angel out of the House: Philanthropy and Gender in Nineteenth-Century England

Richard Maxwell, Editor
The Victorian Illustrated Book

Vineta Colby
Vernon Lee: A Literary Biography

E. Warwick Slinn
Victorian Poetry as Cultural Critique: The Politics of Performative Language

Simon Joyce
Capital Offenses: Geographies of Class and Crime in Victorian London

Caroline Levine
The Serious Pleasures of Suspense: Victorian Realism and Narrative Doubts

Emily Davies
Emily Davies: Collected Letters, 1861–1875
Edited by Ann B. Murphy and Deirdre Raftery

Joseph Bizup
Manufacturing Culture: Vindications of Early Victorian Industry

Lynn M. Voskuil
Acting Naturally: Victorian Theatricality and Authenticity

Sally Mitchell
Frances Power Cobbe: Victorian Feminist, Journalist, Reformer

Constance W. Hassett
Christina Rossetti: The Patience of Style

Brenda Assael
The Circus and Victorian Society

Judith Wilt
Behind Her Times: Transition England in the Novels of Mary Arnold Ward

Daniel Hack
The Material Interests of the Victorian Novel

Frankie Morris
Artist of Wonderland: The Life, Political Cartoons, and Illustrations of Tenniel

William R. McKelvy
The English Cult of Literature: Devoted Readers, 1774–1880

Linda M. Austin
Nostalgia in Transition, 1780–1917

James Buzard, Joseph W. Childers, and Eileen Gillooly, Editors
Victorian Prism: Refractions of the Crystal Palace

Michael Field
The Fowl and the Pussycat: Love Letters of Michael Field, 1876–1909
Edited by Sharon Bickle

Dallas Liddle
The Dynamics of Genre: Journalism and the Practice of Literature in Mid-Victorian Britain

Christine L. Krueger
Reading for the Law: British Literary History and Gender Advocacy

Marjorie Wheeler-Barclay
The Science of Religion in Britain, 1860–1915

Carolyn Betensky
Feeling for the Poor: Bourgeois Compassion, Social Action, and the Victorian Novel

John O. Jordan
Supposing "Bleak House"